To Anne and Dennis
With happy memories of the
holidays and your support
which carried us through

Keeping the Story Alive

Brian Brown
5.3.01

Keeping the Story Alive

Brian D. Brown

paternoster
press

First Published in 2000 by Paternoster Press

06 05 04 03 02 01 00   7 6 5 4 3 2 1
Paternoster Press is an imprint of Paternoster Publishing,
PO Box 300, Carlisle, Cumbria, CA3 0QS, UK
and Paternoster Publishing USA
Box 1047, Waynesboro, GA 30830–2047
www.paternoster-publishing.com

British Library Cataloguing in Publication Data

A catalogue record for this book is available from
The British Library

ISBN 1-84227-029-X

The Choice was first published in 1970 by the National Christian
Education Council; Storyboards in Appendix C
by John Halas © Flame Communications Ltd.

Cover design by Mainstream
Typeset by WestKey, Falmouth
Printed in Great Britain by
Cox and Wyman, Cardiff Road, Reading,
Berkshire RG1 8EX

For my son Paul.
Not a Peter by name.
But always a rock of support.

Contents

Acknowledgments

In the summer of 1998 I visited my old friend Rev. Donald English with whom I had been ordained 36 years previously. He was in hospital in Oxford recovering from heart surgery. As I was leaving, he said quietly and earnestly: 'Brian, you have made a great contribution. The church will always associate you with *The Story Keepers*. Write your story. It needs to be told.' Sadly, he died not long afterwards. He was not only a friend. He was twice President of the Methodist Conference and a great church leader. I had to ponder his words carefully.

In the November of that year I was honoured to receive an invitation from Ms Rachel Viney, at that time the Religious Broadcasting Officer of the Independent Television Commission, on behalf of the organising committee of the European Broadcasting Union Conference 'Religion 99', to give a presentation on my work on *The Story Keepers*. 'We would like to hear how the project came into being,' she wrote, 'how long it took to get off the ground and what your failures and successes were along the way. What lessons have you learned from your experience and what advice would you pass on to religious programme makers struggling (in many cases) to retain audiences in today's competitive broadcasting environment?'

In accepting the invitation I did so on behalf of the many like Donald who had prayerfully watched my ten-year struggle to bring the story of Jesus to the television screen, and who for so long had, at meetings or in private, urged me to tell my story. I had agreed with Pieter Kwant and Mark Finnie of Paternoster to publish the lecture I was to deliver. But up to the Conference in October 1999, at so prestigious an event, before so many influential broadcasters, I was still hesitant about going into the more personal areas Donald English had suggested.

My hesitations were eased when a man with a familiar face and voice stood up as I finished my presentation, and thanked me for persevering with my vision and bringing it to reality. Afterwards the encouragement of this man, Dermod McCarthy, Head of Religious Broadcasting at RTE in Ireland, and of many other broadcasters at the conference led me to think again of Donald English's words: 'Write your story.' I returned to delve into my voluminous files and records of the triumphs and failures, successes and disasters during those ten momentous years in my life as *The Story Keepers* evolved.

I decided not to write a blow-by-blow, historical account of the ups and downs of the saga of those years. I have rather tried to answer Rachel Viney's questions about the evolution of the series and its impact by putting them into a wider social, educational and cultural context of the church's mission to contemporary society. Inevitably, because I have been involved as a teacher, lecturer and preacher in that mission, much of what follows is autobiographical and reflects my ministry, preoccupations and perspective.

I am grateful to Mark and Pieter for encouraging me to open up, and to Nigel Halliday for so carefully editing my prose. But, principally, because she has been centrally involved as my partner and support not only through every stage of the creation of the series but throughout my ministry, I owe a debt to my wife,

Pearl. She has assisted me in my selection of material and in the thrust of my presentation. She taught me the practical meaning of Jesus' words, 'The truth will make you free', and I am grateful for her critical and insightful comments and advice. However, I must take responsibility for the final product. It is my story, as Donald suggested. But in many respects it will always be our story.

Prologue:
A parable for our time

I can still see Paddy now quite clearly. He had been fidgeting in his seat impatiently for the past half hour or so. Now it had got too much. He rose and looked around at his fellow 15-year-old school-leavers. Then he turned a disdainful eye upon the array of clergy displayed before him – the Methodist minister, the Baptist pastor, the Salvation Army officer, the Anglican vicar, the Roman Catholic priest, sitting on the school-hall platform in the conventional position, six feet above contradiction. I feared the worst and realised then that my first instincts had been right. I should never have listened to the group of teachers with whom I had planned the school-leavers' conference. I had wanted to look at the real issues facing the one hundred or so Fourth Year secondary students who would be attending. I suggested 'Getting on with People', 'Making Choices', 'Having Aims in Life', 'School to Work' – the usual adolescent pre-work, pre-adulthood themes. These themes had gone down well in other cities, where, as Secretary for Younger School-Leavers, I had organised the Student Christian Movement in Schools programme.

But who was I to argue with the teachers? A mere stripling of 26, barely out of college, only recently ordained: full of enthusiasm but lacking in experience. What could I say when they meaningfully and over-sympathetically told me at the planning meeting: 'You must remember this is Liverpool. We are planning a *Christian* conference. They [the school-leavers] would expect something on the church.' After all, they said, it was 1963. After Vatican II they will want to talk about Church Unity.

I was not convinced. At the end of their school life, on the cusp of the adventure of adulthood, earning a living, having the legendary discretionary spending – and they would want to talk about Christian Unity? They were expected to talk about warring church traditions and divided congregations! But I duly gave in and when Paddy looked around and began to speak I knew I had made an error.

The 15-year-old Liverpudlian, pulling himself to his full height, stared at the startled clergy who had, for the previous half hour, been soporifically answering polite questions from their young audience which, whilst enjoying a day off from lessons, was now, at 2.15, ready for the streets.

'I'll tell you about Church Unity,' Paddy began with a wry smile. 'We get on fine with the Prots. They get on fine with us. You see we have one thing in common. We don't understand our priests and they don't understand theirs.' As he sat down, the 'Amen to that' from his fellow students could be heard all over Liverpool.

I do not know whether Paddy meant to influence anyone by what he said. I have never forgotten his devastating analysis.

In later years as a researcher, teacher and academic with a particular interest in mission to the industrial working class I read, and like many others was disturbed and challenged by, Ted Wickham's study *Church and People in an Industrial City*.[1] Its thesis is an amplification of an earlier remark by A. F. Winnington in 1896, at a time of arguably the most favourable period for church allegiance in modern times: 'It is not that the Church of

---

[1] E. R. Wickham, *Church and People in an Industrial City* (Lutterworth Press, 1957).

God has lost the great towns; it never had them in the first place.' Reading that and other sociological and cultural studies on the same lines, I came to accept as axiomatic the physical if not also the spiritual alienation of large tracts of the populace in our industrial towns from the institutional organised church.

But no one expressed that alienation so movingly or heartbreakingly succinctly as that unknown Liverpudlian in his last days in a secondary school in the Beatles' Liverpool of the 1960s. I still hear his voice and the echoing 'Amen!' all these years later.

Chapter 1

'If our mum could see him now . . .'

My first three days in the Harefield Hostal were a complete blur. I had been admitted to the John Radcliffe Hospital in Oxford on the Thursday before Holy Week in 1983. The cardiac consultant whom I had seen in out-patients for recurrent and persistent sharp chest pain had asked me if I could stay a couple of days to allow for tests, observation and, in her words, 'to see what is really going on'.

Six weeks previously I had undergone an angiogram in order, as the cardiologist put it, 'to set your mind and ours to rest'. But the results did nothing of the kind: I had three blocked arteries, and one was blocking fast. I did not really know what that meant but I agreed to wait quietly at home until I was called for by-pass surgery: the waiting list was six months. So when the cardiologist asked to admit me to hospital for a couple of days of tests, I saw no reason to question or to suspect that I might be critically ill.

The Friday was an unreal dream. I counted seven clergy at my bedside, including the Chairman of the Oxford and Leicester District of the Methodist Church, who travelled over forty miles from Northampton, two Methodist Superintendent ministers, an Anglican vicar, a Catholic priest and two other fellow Methodist ministers. I cannot recall who brought me the bread and wine, and I was too dazed to say no when they offered to pray and celebrate communion. I had myself been a hospital chaplain, and in my 25 or more years as a minister I had visited many seriously ill patients. So I knew what bed rest implied; I knew what intravenous medication suggested. But I had no idea that my unstable condition was giving rise to the kind of anxiety my colleagues clearly must have felt.

The house doctor informed me on the Friday evening that there was good news: a bed had suddenly become available at the Harefield Hospital and my operation was being brought forward. But still it did not sink in. I was whisked away the following day to the Harefield and placed in the care of Professor Yacoub and his famous heart team. I was immediately put on a drip again and eventually went down to the theatre for the coronary bypass at 8.30 a.m. on the Tuesday morning. In the early 1980s coronary artery bypass surgery was relatively in its infancy and took far longer than it does now. It was almost 36 hours later when I came round in my cubicle ward after a quadruple bypass.

I remember little of that first Wednesday. I know my wife and two of my sisters were there because, in my semi-awake state, I overheard a snatch of conversation. My younger sister turned to my elder sister and whispered words I was to mull over during the next weeks: 'If our mum could see him now . . .'

The next day one of the seniors in the surgical team came to see me. In a matter-of-fact, almost cheerful and triumphant voice, he told me, 'When we operated, we discovered that you were getting no blood to one side of your heart and scarcely any to the other.' He added the startling truth which my colleagues must have guessed and I had not even suspected: 'Consider yourself a lucky chap. By rights you could – probably should – have died at any time during the past three and a half years. You could have been driving down a motorway, had a massive fatal heart attack and no one would have known any more. But you'll be fine now. You could outlive us all.' I have not spoken to that doctor, or any other of Professor Yacoub's team, since the operation; but they have as much to do with *The Story Keepers* appearing on television screens all around the world as anybody.

The Sunday of that first week was Easter Day and I went down to communion in the small hospital chapel. The reading was the Easter story of Mary's encounter with Jesus in the Garden of Gethsemane following the resurrection. I noted that Jesus addressed Mary by name.

I went back to my cubicle and thought of the words of the surgeon: 'You're a lucky chap.' I asked myself: Why was I lucky? Why was I not another unexplained cardiac statistic? I could make no sense of it. I had none of the factors that doctors say are the cause of the chronic disease which clogged up my coronary arteries. I had never smoked. I had not touched alcohol for almost 30 years. My blood cholesterol was low. My blood pressure was normal and, as far as I knew, there was no history of heart disease in the family.

It seemed grossly unfair. I was forty-seven. My elder daughter was just about to sit her finals at college. I had three other children of secondary age. I figured I had at least another 25 or 30 years of active life ahead of me. Yet here I was snatched from death only because of advances in medical science: ten or even five years before I might well have died a 'premature' death.

Then I thought of that reading at Easter communion in the chapel. Jesus said: 'Mary.' Her life had been shattered; her hopes destroyed; her future blighted. But Jesus addressed her by name and gave her instructions: 'Go to my brothers and tell them.'[1] I lay musing over those words for hours on end.

My nurse came in and asked: 'Is there anything you want, Reverend Brown?' Later another came in and asked me: 'What do you want for lunch, Mr Brown?' The formality of address came as no surprise. Before the 'touchy feelie' nineties, nursing staff still addressed male patients in the traditional, stiff forms. In the fourteen days I was in the Harefield no one called me anything except Mr or Reverend. No one? Not quite.

---

[1] John 20:16.

From the time of my pre-med and falling asleep on my bed at 8.30 a.m. on the Tuesday morning until I came around in my room and overheard my sisters talking to my wife the following evening, I can remember only one thing. But it was so vivid I can almost hear it now. Someone, during the hours when I was hovering between life and death, when my heart was stopped and its function taken over by an artificial heart–lung machine; someone, when I was 'dead', spoke my name: 'Brian! Brian!' Not 'Mr Brown' or 'Reverend' but my Christian name. The name by which I was known by those who loved me and cared for me in my family before and after I married.

When I was helpless, when I was dead, I was addressed. I was 'called' by name. I was loved. I was cared for. I was needed for service. There was a reason why I had avoided early death from heart attack. There was a reason why I had been snatched from death.

I thought of John Wesley snatched from the flames of the vicarage at Epworth. I too was a 'brand snatched from the burning,' as he and his brother Charles sang later. It sounds almost impious, let alone presumptuous, to speak of my life and work in the same breath as the founders of the movement and ministry into which I had been ordained. But 14 years later, on 14 January 1997, as I waited for *The Story Keepers* to appear on television for the first time, I thought of those words: 'If our mum could see him now . . .' She would have been proud of her little lad. But, like me, she would have been grateful that he was alive to see the day.

I thought of Paddy, my unknown school-leaver in Liverpool whose words I had recalled as I lay recovering in hospital. The 14 years after I left the Harefield had been devoted, as had the previous 40, to the likes of Paddy and my mum. *The Story Keepers* was for them and marked the summation of my esoteric and unconventional ministry.

Chapter 2

From the boundary

Heart patients, particularly men, will understand that the days following heart surgery are emotionally draining. After years of keeping the upper lip stiff, those of us brought up to play the traditional English macho role find it difficult to weep openly. It is hard to come to terms with uncontrollable, involuntary tears which pour down the face when watching even the most innocuous television play or film, or worse, sobbing at the sight of loved ones. Even the consoling shoulder of the nurse, and her assurances that weeping is quite natural after all the shocks the body has taken, do little to dispel the sheer bewilderment of the emotional shock That is particularly so if, like me, you have lived a public life as a minister in which you have shared others' experiences of pain, sorrow, death and fear, and were always expected to be strong: yours were the shoulders others cried upon.

I was no exception, and wept many tears for many hours. To this day my elder son, in his early teens when I was ill, wonders what he had done to cause me to have one of my weepy bouts every time he walked into the ward. But in between the times of emotional release there was opportunity to look back on events and people in my personal history, and to reassess my future.

When I was researching for my first master's thesis at the University of Birmingham in 1968 Dan Hardy, my American tutor and subsequently, a friend to whom I am greatly indebted, introduced me to the collected writings of Paul Tillich. His was a name I had first met, along with those of Bonhoeffer and Bultmann, in 1963 when, as a member of the Student Christian Movement staff, I was sent a copy of John Robinson's epoch-making book *Honest to God*[1] a month before its publication. As a result of Robinson's book we all read Tillich's *Shaking of the Foundations*, and I dipped into the second volume of his *Systematic Theology*[2]

I had graduated in theology in 1960 after three years' training for the Methodist ministry at Handsworth Theological College, Birmingham: prior to that I had graduated in modern history from the University of Bristol in 1957. I was now familiar with all the disputes of the Early Church, and I knew my Greek and Hebrew critical Biblical studies. But, although the writings of the continental theologians whom John Robinson discussed in his little book had been around for a long time, they came almost as a shock to me at first. I remember railing against Tillich, Bonhoeffer and particularly Bultmann in the staff conferences and meetings held to discuss the implications of the book. But I never really *read* any of their original works until I began to research with Dan Hardy.

There is much with which I still fail to empathise in Tillich's works. Much of it I find philosophically hard to enter. But one of his themes which I read in 1968 struck a chord with me. He talks of his role as a Christian theologian addressing Marxism, Freudianism and Existentialism from a position he describes as being 'on the boundary'.[3] When I read these words six years after I was ordained, and when I recalled them later as I reviewed my ministry from my hospital bed, and as I do so now in my study, I was struck by how closely Tillich's stance seems to apply to the

---

[1] John T. Robinson, *Honest to God* (SCM Press, 1963).

[2] Paul Tillich, *The Shaking of the Foundations* (SCM Press, 1949); *Systematic Theology*, Vol. 2 (Nisbet, 1957).

[3] Paul Tillich, *Protestant Era* (Phoenix Books, 1957); *On the Boundary* (Collins, 1967).

work I have been doing since I walked out of theological college for the last time.

Sitting in lectures or in my college study I had no thought that a ministry outside the normal Methodist Circuit structures might lie ahead. No one talked of anything but the pastoral, preaching ministry of the Circuit minister travelling around the Methodist Connexion. After receiving a traditional training I went into the Hunts Mission Circuit in Huntingdon in 1960 fully expecting 40 years on to have 'travelled', as we Methodists say, from Circuit to Circuit every four to five years. I anticipated conducting weddings, baptisms and funerals, endless meetings and Sunday services, making pastoral calls on my members and living the normal, ordered life of service to the church and community of the Methodist Circuit minister. In the 1950s few Methodist ministers worked outside the Circuit structures. After my hectic two years' probation in Huntingdon, I began a four-year post-ordination stint with Student Christian Movement in Schools. But I had reason to think that, following this, I would settle down as a circuit minister.

However, it was because of the many young people like Paddy whom I met in schools across the country during those four years with SCM that my ministry was to be directed towards where he and they were – outside the formal structures of the organised churches. It was for them that I was to take up, for the next 38 years, a position 'on the boundary'.

SCM in Schools worked with students in the final years of secondary modern education, but our brief was never specified. We described it generally as seeking to redeem the image of religion for young people in schools; or, in our less cynical moments, we said we were making the Christian faith socially relevant to the lives of boys and girls. The local authorities, who financed our work, and the teachers who co-operated with us, saw the young men and women of SCM in Schools' staff as helping disaffected young people find some purpose in their lives which might help them in the troublesome transition from school to work.

Whether we achieved any of those laudable goals I do not know. What the attempts to reach them in those four years did for me I do know.

As a young minister I represented the organised church to the groups from schools who attended our day or weekend conferences, festivals, courses and work camps. Having grown up in a working-class area of Bristol with a father who was a dock-worker, and coming to Christian faith and becoming part of the church only as a student at university, I should have been forewarned of the cultural gap between Paddy and his friends and the church. But I was no more prepared for the depth of the alienation than were my Home Counties suburban clergy colleagues or the other ministers with whom I was working. It did not, however, take me long to realise that I represented an alien culture, lifestyle, belief-system and institution.

The experience of separation of language, attitudes and behaviour I encountered between Monday and Saturday was heightened by Sunday preaching services held in various churches across the North-West. At first the Sundays were a relief, a spiritual retreat to fortify the batteries. Later they were a troublesome, disturbing escape. With few exceptions, the young people and their families with whom I worked on weekdays were singularly absent from Sunday services, and not part of the monochrome social group which made up my congregations. They had been absent for most of their growing lives and would, except for the then obligatory rites of passage, be separated from the church-attending groups for the rest of their lives. They were unused to the rituals, signs and symbols of worship and were unfamiliar with the language of prayer, sermons, hymns and above all biblical readings. Although we made valiant efforts in our SCM in Schools group meetings and our weekend conferences to introduce people to biblical stories and passages, we did not need researchers to tell us the brutal fact that we could not assume that the young people present were familiar with the language and the thought forms in which Christian faith was expressed.

We gave sound theological reasons to teachers who queried whether a day conference, in which the Bible was hardly, if ever, mentioned and in which Biblical stories and language were not used, could be called a Christian conference. We recognised from experience that growing up in homes where the Bible was seldom opened, let alone read, where discussion about Christian issues was, at best, rare, where the language and practice of prayer was more often absent than present, and where the members were cut off from the communities which used religious language and read biblical words, most of the urban young people with whom we worked would not have been able to confer with us, had we not talked about adolescence-based, apparently secular topics. If we had used biblical or traditional Church language no discussion would have been possible.

In my SCM in Schools days I had vaguely heard of, but not read, the work of Basil Bernstein focusing on the difficulties many working-class children have in acquiring literacy skills and the language appropriate to book-based learning. Relative to children who have access to a range of books in their homes, made available to them from the cradle by adults who value books and read them to children and who use structured formal language favoured in schools, they are, he said in the language favoured at the time, 'disadvantaged'.[4] But we did not need academic research to tell us that, in the same way, these same working-class young people, if they did not have access to the Bible or move in the circles where biblical language and stories were read and valued, would simply not be able to converse with us if we used the kind of language used in the churches.

I for one was too immersed in the mission tasks we had been given to be asking, let alone considering, research questions. Organising, and more often than not leading, up to three full conferences each week for three terms, plus summer camps, a

[4] Basil Bernstein, *Class Codes and Control*, Vol. 1 (Routledge & Kegan Paul, 1971), p. 42, 61ff.

spell as a chaplain to a pop group agency in Manchester, work in the Cavern Club, Liverpool and writing a weekly teenagers' column for an evening newspaper, left little time to reflect.

Every day of those four years, the praxis of engagement raised the same questions and challenges that I was to address for the rest of my ministry; and, as I considered my future in the Harefield 17 years later, they came to me again. How do we reach the likes of Paddy? How do we bridge the gulf between the churched and the unchurched? How do we communicate biblical stories and truths to those I later came to term the 'biblically illiterate'? From my position on the boundary, outside the church's structures, what was I called to do?

The author welcomes David Frost at an SCM in Schools Festival in 1964. Frost was at that time known for presenting television's satirical *That Was the Week That Was*.

Chapter 3

Participation in the situation

I am not a natural academic. I do not enjoy researching for its own sake. I must have a reason, questions I must answer. The four years in Lancashire threw up enough questions to last a lifetime.

I also need a stimulator. Alan Dale, Methodist Minister, biblical translator and teacher and, for one unforgettable year my Head of Department when I was appointed to be Number Three in the Religious Studies Department of Dudley College of Education, was my stimulator. During that year he was completing his translation of the New Testament for young people, published initially in five volumes under the title *New World*.[1] Written first for his own students and then for teachers, *New World* and the follow-on translation of the Old Testament, *Winding Quest*, became bestsellers and essential materials for primary and secondary teachers and church educators.

Alan was one of the quartet of innovators in religious education in the 1960s who had profound effects upon all involved in communicating to the young, and upon me in particular. The others were Douglas Hubery, a fellow Methodist minister who, like me, worked outside the church for many years; Harold

---

[1] Alan T. Dale, *New World* (Oxford University Press, 1967); *Winding Quest* (Oxford University Press, 1972).

Loukes from Oxford and Ronald Goldman from Reading, with both of whom I worked in my Student Christian Movement days.[2] From different perspectives, the four of them called for a new approach to religious education. They all took seriously the dashed hopes and sense of failure, felt and expressed by teachers, concerning the clause in the 1944 Education Act which enshrined the teaching of religion in the school curriculum. All four recognised the naïveté of the assumption made by the compilers of the Agreed Syllabuses of Religious Education, issued during the previous 20 years, that if Bible stories and teaching were taught by professional teachers as a compulsory element of the state-school curriculum (religious education was at that time the only compulsory subject) for the minimum ten school years, they would be learned and absorbed by even non-church-going 'Paddy's. They all four acknowledged that Bonhoeffer had been percipient in suggesting in his *Letters and Papers from Prison*[3] that during and after the war the drift away of masses of people, not only from the churches as institutions themselves, but from religion itself, would mean that society, as it was emerging, was 'radically without religion'.

All four argued that a new approach was required. Douglas Hubery talked of an 'experiential approach', teaching from the experience of the teacher and from that of the Bible to the experience of the children. Loukes and Goldman talked of exploring the grand themes of the Bible and relating them to the lives of the students. Alan Dale told his student teachers: 'Start where they are. Take them back to the Bible and bring them back to the present.'

---

[2] Douglas Hubery, *The Experiential Approach to Christian Education* (National Sunday School Union, 1960) Harold Loukes, *Teenage Religion* (SCM Press, 1959) Ronald Goldman, *Religious Thinking From Childhood to Adolescence* (Routledge & Kegan Paul, 1964).

[3] Dietrich Bonhoeffer, *Letters and Papers from Prison* (Fontana Books, 1959).

To help his students understand where the young are, Alan organised field courses introducing his students to studies of society and group structures, and he encouraged them and his colleagues in the department to understand the nature of contemporary culture. He encouraged me to try to make sense of the issues and questions I had encountered during my four years' work with school-leavers in Lancashire, and he was instrumental in my making an approach to do research for a master's degree at the University of Birmingham. Here I spent three years writing a thesis on theology and working-class culture, while also holding down a teaching post at Dudley College of Education.

Alan's greatest contribution, however, was to acknowledge that the teacher could raise and explore all the issues in the world, but unless he or she could put in the hands of the children a translation of the biblical stories that the young could read, appropriate and understand, no communication of the truths of the Bible could take place. Alan could endorse Paul Tillich's graphic aphorism that true communication comes from participation in the situation and being critically engaged in dialogue. But he contended that the teacher needed to have the tools to engage in critical dialogue. These he sought to provide in *New World* and *Winding Quest*, and he encouraged me to provide more in the workbooks to his translation, *The Choice* and *The Search*[4] which I eventually published in 1970, three years after he retired.

New World and *Winding Quest* were eye-openers for me. But so too were the many hours I spent talking to the great teacher and learning his craft. Alan was a poet and a hymn writer, and he had a beautiful, elegant but simple writing style for children. I often wish more teachers and clergy had had the benefit of his tutorials, so that the true value of this set of books might be appreciated more widely. For they were not only attractively presented with beautiful illustrations, they were also written in

---

[4] Brian Brown, *The Choice* (Denholm House/E. J. Arnold, 1970); *The Search* (Denholm House/E. J. Arnold, 1970).

contemporary language, neither in the grandeur of seventeenth-century 'Thees and Thous' and 'Here Beginneths', nor, as he naughtily pointed out, like the recently published *New English Bible*, in the language of *The Times*. He chose the pithy, earthy language of the prince of tabloids, *The Daily Mirror*: 'That's the language Mark certainly chose to use,' Alan often said. One-verb sentences. Few qualifiers. Action not verbiage. The language of the common folk. The common language. The koine. And, as I came to see, the language of Paddy and his friends. Recognising that, as children mature, so their reading age develops, Alan graded his New Testament translation through the five volumes, telling the story of Jesus in Mark with language suitable for the child with a reading age of 9; the teaching and parables for reading age 10; the story of Jesus in Luke and Luke–Acts for reading age 11; the story of Paul for reading age 12; and the more difficult writings of Paul and those of John for reading age 13, the average reading age of most people.

Although Alan carefully chose the words of his translation to communicate to those who were not familiar with the traditional language used in churches, he did not flinch from meeting head-on the challenges of biblical scholarship. His second favourite maxim was: 'Never be afraid of scholarship.' Angered by what he saw as the moral cowardice of teachers and clergy who, as soon as they stepped out of the study and stood in front of a class or a congregation, promptly put aside all they had learned from the scholars, Alan urged us to be bold. Without making a fuss, or even telling anyone, he based his young person's translation on the best available, up-to-date scholarship, incorporating in his selection, ordering and presentation of New Testament stories and teaching the work of Source Historical and Form Historical critics, and the work of great British scholars, like T. W. Manson on the historical Jesus and C. H. Dodd on the structure of the Gospel of John. Had he made a fuss, the critics would have screamed that he was confusing or undermining the young. That so few of them recognised the depth of the scholarship which led him to omit the nativity stories and the so-called 'Church words' at the end of well-known parables such as the parable of the Sower, or to place John's Gospel at the end of the collection after the epistles of Paul, is tribute to his subtlety as well as his bravery.

The exquisitely elegant arrangement of his Old Testament translation, beginning, as most scholars would but no other translations had dared, with the earliest history – the stories of the kings of Israel – and ending with those who tried to make sense of the story of the people of God, may well have been overlooked owing to the great success of its predecessor. But its impact on me was no less strong. The seeds of the approach to Bible story-telling I used in *The Story Keepers*, aiming to speak in language understandable by my friend Paddy and not hiding from him the findings of scholarship, were sown in those hours with Alan Dale. They bore fruit in my translations of those same stories into animation 25 years later.

As I lay in hospital thinking of my future work and role, ten years after Alan's death, his advice would have been the same: 'Start with them. Speak to them in a medium with which they are familiar. Explore real experiences of people living in God's world. Introduce them to Jesus and the men and women of God in the Bible. Help them to see the Bible as a record of real people living in real situations. Take those historical and social situations seriously. Tell the stories in their language. But underpin all you do by scholarship.' There is no doubt that Alan's influence determined the way I was to approach translating and telling Bible stories on television years later.

Chapter 4

'You're Christians, I'm a Communist ...'

Logically, my acceptance in 1971 of the post of Head of Religious Studies at Lady Spencer-Churchill College in Oxford, one of the last small, all-female colleges of education, was an unwise career move. A former colleague from Dudley College of Education, who met me wandering around the opulent new college buildings in lush rural Oxfordshire just before the beginning of my first term, must have noticed the glazed look of cultural bewilderment in my eyes. With a concerned look he asked me if I would really be happy in my new surroundings.

Twelve years later, as I lay musing in my hospital bed, I knew what he meant. 'High Table', coffee in the buttery, and tea each day at four; strawberries and cream on the lawn for Commemoration during Royal Ascot Week, proud parents coming up from the Races for the day; award ceremonies in the Sheldonian; Freshers' coming-up services in the University Church: this was hardly the lifestyle for the son of a docker who went to redbrick universities and would wince when student applicants were asked at interview: 'And what does daddy do, dear?'

I had, after all, worked for the previous nine years with young people in the industrial North-West and the Black Country. I had gone into academia as much to sit back and try to make sense of the questions I had encountered in my work with SCM in Schools, as to teach trainee teachers. I had spent much of the last three years in the University of Birmingham researching working-class life and culture for my thesis on theology and working-class life. I had sat three times a week in seminars with postgraduates from a range of other disciplines in the recently established Centre for Contemporary Cultural Studies. Alongside me in these seminars were two of my intellectual heroes, the brilliant West Indian social analyst Stuart Hall, and Richard Hoggart, the giant of working-class cultural studies and founder of the Centre. Hoggart's epoch-making study of working-class culture, *The Uses of Literacy*,[1] had been my constant companion since I left college.

I had also begun to see a little of what lay behind Paddy's outburst that day in Liverpool. Like Richard Hoggart, I had grown up in a culture which was not merely unlike but miles apart from that in which Christians increasingly felt comfortable. The sociologists I read, such as Thomas O'Dea and Max Weber, and social historians such as R. H. Tawney and my late friend E. R. Wickham, Bishop of Middleton, had talked about the historical alienation from the institutional churches experienced by those, uprooted from rural communities, who emigrated to towns in the early days of industrial Britain. But the work of Hoggart, Hall, Raymond Williams and other cultural analysts focused my attention upon the reality of that alienation for Christian mission 200 years later.

At the beginning of the soccer season in 1957, as I was about to leave Bristol as a new graduate and enter a theological college, I played a farewell match with the Port of Bristol Football Club with which I had played for seven years. Bidding me goodbye, one of my team-mates asked innocently what I was going to do when I went away.

'I'm going into the ministry,' I replied.

'Oh yes, which one?' he said. 'Ministry of Fuel, Food or something like that?' It was not a witticism. It was simply

---

[1] Richard Hoggart, *Uses of Literacy* (Penguin Books, 1958).

inconceivable to him or the others in the wintergreen–smelling dressing-room that the lad they had known for the past seven years would no longer be, in Richard Hoggart's graphic phrase, one of 'Us', the kith, kin, friendship groups on the receiving end of orders and the wrong end of power and its rewards; but that I would become part of the impersonal, anonymous 'Them,' who controlled, made the decisions which affected our lives and had little to do with 'ordinary folk like us'. As I recall the line of clergy dismissed so cheerfully by Paddy, I realise that they represented 'Them'. He was part of 'Us'. As a result of my ordination I became part of 'Them'. Twenty-five years later, the members of the docks football team shook hands with me with genuine pride and affection after I gave the address at my father's funeral. But I was still part of 'Them' because of the cassock and collar I wore.

My own early research in the Centre for Contemporary Cultural Studies was into the lifestyle and world-view which, over the centuries, those feeling comfortable with 'Us' had developed. It focused on issues which were to remain dominant in my later work. There was, first of all, the research of Basil Bernstein and the so-called 'cultural deficists' into what Josephine Klein was to term 'cognitive poverty'.[2] It has been fashionable since the 1970s to downplay this school of thought, and that of the compilers of the Plowden Report,[3] as reverse élitism propagated by those who, having climbed the educational ladder, found themselves socially uprooted and alienated from their background. In some circles it is not politically correct to talk of the cultural deficit of working-class children. But if Tillich is right to say that true communication comes from participation in the situation, and if the cultural situation of those who participate in the church universe is so different from that of working-class communities

---

[2] Josephine Klein, *Samples from English Cultures* (Routledge & Kegan Paul, 1965).
[3] Central Advisory Council for Education, *Children and their Primary Schools* (HMSO, 1967).

outside, then we who wish to communicate the church's historic message to the masses of folk outside have a problem.

That Bernstein, Plowden and others used what is now regarded as offensive language in talking about problems of cultural or, in Klein's case, more unfortunately, *cognitive* deficiency (no one could say that my father, unschooled and untutored though he may have been, was deficient in cognitive capacity), should not detract from the thrust of their genuine concern. The educated classes are in many ways enriched by their access to books and learning and *comparatively* those who have not the same access are impoverished.

My forebears in Methodism had discovered that the message they sang 'for all, for all my saviour died,' was appropriated by those culturally privileged classes and denied to those less privileged; and they were right to seek to remedy the cultural deficit by beginning Sunday Schools and Class meetings so that the poor might be able to read, understand and accept the message. They would have understood the thrust of Dickens' moving but troubling description of Jo from Tom-All-Alone's in *Bleak House*:

> It must be a strange state to be like Jo! To shuffle through the streets, unfamiliar with the shapes, and in utter darkness as to the meaning, of those mysterious symbols, so abundant over the shops, at the corners of streets, and on the doors, and in the windows! To see people read, and to see people write, and to see postmen deliver letters, and not have the least idea of all that language – to be, to every scrap of it, stone blind and dumb! It must be very puzzling to see the good company going to the churches on Sundays, with their books in their hands, and to think (for perhaps Jo does think, at odd times) what does it all mean, and if it means anything to anybody, how comes it that it means nothing to me?

I had not read that passage when, as a young teacher in an all-boys secondary modern school in inner Birmingham during my theological college days, I watched one of my class standing outside the public conveniences. As a man entered, the boy followed. I learned later that he could not read 'Gents' or 'Ladies'. Yet I was seeking to teach him stories from the pages of the Bible!

Alan Dale was in an honourable tradition in his attempt to make biblical stories accessible to children and adults in language they could appropriate. Wyclif, Tyndale and the Protestant Reformers were all motivated by the same vision to bring the biblical story alive for people of all social groups. The drive to spread literacy began with Robert Raikes and the Sunday Schools who wanted the illiterate poor to read the stories of the Bible for themselves. Raikes argued that the illiteracy of Rochdale's poor was denying them access to the Good News. It was to combat biblical illiteracy that the Sunday Schools, both to teach the mechanics of reading and to encourage understanding of the content, were established. These schools held on Sunday, the only day of rest from work in the mills and factories, developed in the nineteenth century to become day schools supported by the churches, and their example was an impetus towards free schooling for all, which was only established in 1944.

The work of Bernstein and others demonstrated for me that the provision of free education for all has not meant that literacy, the entrée to cultural power, has been appropriated by all. Free access to education has not automatically meant free access to the world of books, knowledge and learning. The cruel parody of the former slum-dwellers keeping the coal in the bath of their newly acquired council semi-detached house, hides a bitter reality for those whose hopes were raised by the provision of free educational access. That reality was particularly bitter for those who believed that, once biblical teaching was made compulsory in the post-1944 schools, the nation would become biblically literate and the churches' message would be heard. The compilers of the Plowden Report showed clearly that other factors besides free access to schooling determined whether normally intelligent children would learn to read, or even want to learn to read.

At the beginning of my research, I read, with excitement and with awe, Basil Bernstein's newly published and highly influential work on language.[4] He divided language into two major categories, that which was spoken in the home and playground and that which was spoken in the classroom. The former he called *public* language; the latter, the more structured academic language, he categorised as *formal* language. If the language you hear in the home, he said, aligns itself to that which you hear and require in the classroom, you will more easily acquire the skills to read. But, he said later as he elaborated his argument, if the child hears structured language patterns in the home; if from an early age he engages in structured sentence formation, using elaborated codes of language; if he sees books around him as he grows; if books and learning are respected by those who are opinion-leaders to him; if he sees books read; if he hears books and stories read to him from the cradle: then he is not only more able to become literate but more able to develop the distinctive skills which lead to understanding what is read and to engagement with it. Or, as Ronald Goldman put it, he is more likely to be able to think abstractly and propositionally. When that happens, the whole world of knowledge, learning, and imagination is open to him. I took Bernstein's message seriously: when a child possesses only a public language, when the language code he uses is restricted, he will not possess the necessary tools to seize the opportunities offered.

I took equally seriously what Ian Ramsey said about the language I was primarily interested in, *religious* language.[5] This was, he said, special language. It is the language used in prayer and worship and comes alive and takes on meaning within a religious community. The stories of the Bible, using biblical language, are also '*special*' in this same sense. They are heard, come alive and

---

[4] Basil Bernstein, *Class Codes and Control*, Vol. 1 (Routledge & Kegan Paul, 1971), pp. 42–5.

[5] Ian T. Ramsey, *Religious Language* (SCM, 1957), pp. 19ff.

take meaning within the Christian community, the church. When a child possesses the equivalent of public religious language it is rather a lot to expect him to listen to and appropriate stories and teaching couched in the equivalent of formal religious language.

Bernstein and Ramsey helped me to understand why even Alan Dale's carefully phrased stories, graded by reading age, would be difficult to grasp for young people who were outside the religious communities. There is alongside literacy, I learned, biblical literacy and its corollary, *biblical* illiteracy. Biblical literacy is acquired in the same way as all forms of literacy, by hearing biblical stories, hearing biblical language spoken in the home, being surrounded by Bibles and by adults who legitimate the Bible, and by association with the community in which the Bible is read and venerated, the church. Without these foundation-building experiences in the environment in which he is acculturated, the young child will grow relatively biblically impoverished and biblically illiterate.

This had, indeed, been my own experience. As an undergraduate history student coming fresh to worship and the life of the Christian community, I had discovered that I was, despite all the other academic skills at my disposal, illiterate biblically. I, like most in the working-class communities with which I am familiar, lacked the special literacy skills which are necessary to hear, read or understand the language in which the stories of the Christian religion are couched. As a literate person I could decode the letters to make them into words, sentences and paragraphs. But even in the most modern translations available to me in 1954, Moffatt and Phillips, I could not appropriate the content of what I was reading.

Biblical illiteracy was the problem, it seemed to me, which the increasing secularisation of society and the alienation of large numbers from the church were presenting to those of us who wished to communicate the Christian biblical message. True communication comes not just from participation in the situation, but from ensuring that all those involved have the special literacy skills to participate in the dialogue.

The situation has been further complicated by the new factor to which the Centre for Contemporary Cultural Studies was drawing attention, the end of the dominance of print media – or what Marshall McLuhan was calling in the 1960s, the end of 'The Gutenberg Galaxy'.[6] As if the recognition of the cultural gulf between the churches and the mass of the young with their resulting biblical illiteracy were not enough to undermine the church's assumptions about its audience for mission, the arrival of television as a cultural transformer was to change everything.

Less than 15 years before I joined the Centre, television had 'arrived' with the coronation and the 1954 football world cup. Hoggart's previous work had focused on the influence of *Peg's Paper*, *Red Letter Weekly* and the popular press in forming the distinctive culture in which he and I grew up. Now that culture was increasingly influenced by the new electronic media, and television in particular. Research into television was in its infancy in Britain, but I had seen sufficient to convince me that, if I were to find any way to bridge the cultural gap between the churches and the mass of the people and to counter their biblical illiteracy, I should have to take the possibilities of television seriously.

A college on the edge of Oxford hardly seemed the right place to do that. I could not have been further wrong as events transpired.

Fifteen years later, in 1986, just after I retired from academic work and was considering how to diversify my interests, an incident brought home to me the significance of the biblical illiteracy of a whole generation. I was in a meeting in Paris with a group of television producers and writers. The head of one of the French television children's departments was telling of a visit her daughter had made with a group of other students to Moscow. It

---

[6] See Marshall McLuhan, *Understanding Media* (Ark, 1964), and *The Medium is the Massage* (Penguin, 1967).

was then still under the old régime. The students were being given the usual tourist visit to one of the great Moscow churches and the guide was enthusiastically explaining the stories behind the biblical pictures on the walls. Seeing that his guests were fascinated, the guide turned to them and said in surprise: 'You're Christians, I'm a Communist. But I know the Bible stories and you don't.' I am sure that both the guide and the woman television executive would have been astonished to know that their words would lead me to *The Story Keepers*.

David Frost addresses the SCM in Schools Festival, 1964.

Chapter 5

Modular man

At the Prague European Broadcasting Union Conference 'Religion 99' which I addressed in October 1999, sixteen years after my bypass operation, I was asked by one European religious broadcaster, in his very careful and precise English: 'How is it that you, an ordinary Methodist minister with no specific training in television production, no support from large media organisations, and no capital, have been able to achieve what we broadcasters with all our advantages have sought but failed to do?'

I burbled an embarrassed answer which the very serious-minded questioner found quite unhelpful. But I could not answer that question even if I had had two hours to do so. The best I could have offered would have been to talk *modular*.

Arriving in Oxford in 1971 to take up my post at Lady Spencer-Churchill College, I would not have thought of myself as a 'modular man', even if I had heard the expression. But I had not then read Alvin Toffler's insightful study *Future Shock*,[1] which had been published in the UK the year before.

Toffler bases his thesis upon the received wisdom of sociologists such as Peter Drucker[2] that change as a constant would be the feature of the coming post-industrial society. In the book,

[1] Alvin Toffler, *Future Shock* (Pan Books, 1970).
[2] Peter Drucker, *The Age of Discontinuity* (Pan Books, 1969).

which I read for the first time in 1973, Toffler goes a step further in saying that by-products of change – redundancy, obsolescence, transience, transitoriness – would produce a new mutation, a new kind of animal whom Toffler dubbed 'modular man'. Continually on the move from job to job, never settling in one occupation or trade or profession, modular man, Toffler argues, sees his career not as a linear process by which he works his way up within his chosen trade or profession, but as a set of discontinued, nebulously connected, finished experiences which he sets aside with an alacrity bordering on the callous.

As I ruminated on my career path from 1960 to my hospital bed in 1983, I could see that I fitted Toffler's model frighteningly accurately. That was *my* history. I seemed to be multi-man to colleagues who watched, I am sure with a mixture of disbelief and despair, as I seemed to eschew the conventional teaching and research pattern in one field, flitting from interest to interest like an academic butterfly, never settling, and moving on when the work had barely begun. It is true that I was intellectually restless. But there was one thread of continuity – my concern for mission to working-class children. I was searching all the time for a way of bridging the gap between the kids in our secondary schools and the Christian message, the gap which had haunted me since my SCM in Schools days.

I did not at first choose to become the modular man that I ended up lecturing about. But during the 1970s my career pattern became a visible demonstration of the rationale of the modular degree course which students in the newly enlarged Oxford Polytechnic, to whom I lectured from 1975 to 1986, were meant to experience in their education. I lived the modular lifestyle for which our degree programme was meant to prepare them. However, although I did not set out to be multi-man by choice, I used the changes in my work pattern, with all the accompanying upheavals in my academic life, to achieve that over-riding goal, finding that way of communicating the Bible stories to the unchurched.

Just as I seemed, in 1971, to have arrived in a secure, moderately well-paid job with twenty years' untouchable tenure ahead of me, the higher education revolution exploded. Within a term of arriving at Lady Spencer-Churchill College, at my third academic board meeting, I was listening to one of Her Majesty's Inspectors informing us that, as a result of changes in higher education to be announced by the government, the college would cease to be independent and would be swallowed up by – or, in the polite jargon of the time, 'amalgamated with' – Oxford Polytechnic, the large institution nearby. So much for my vision of living out my career in one job in Oxford!

However, a number of things seemed to come together, and I grabbed the opportunity to branch out in a variety of directions, diversifying my interests and my academic research in ways which directly prepared me for my work on *The Story Keepers*. A part-time theological consultancy in the Luton Industrial College from 1973 to 1978 enabled me, through courses for young people and for industrial workers, to develop further my academic interests in mission to the industrial working class and to contemporary youth culture. Then in 1976 there was an invitation to be one of the first group of postgraduate students on a new course in religion and humanism in the Department of Theology in Birmingham, which I had left only five years before. This enabled me to deepen my interest in religion and culture with a study of the history of Methodism and the working class in mining areas. The withering away of theology as an academic discipline at Oxford Polytechnic, and the need to diversify into the Sociology of Education to meet changed teaching requirements, led me to spend a further year researching the Sociology of Education and Mass Communications in the Centre for Mass Communications Research at Leicester.

It was at Leicester towards the end of the 1970s that the two driving forces in my academic and evangelistic life came together – the cultural significance of television in contemporary society, and the significance for communicators of the work of sociologists such as Bernstein and Halsey on language in the home, school and society. For the troublesome, embarrassing questions raised for communicators and teachers by the sociologists of education and the sociologists of media in the 1970s are not unique to Christian communicators. We are not the only ones in our rapidly changing intellectual and social universe who are continually having to play 'catch up' as we try to find ways of adapting the message to new media.

The irony of Alan Dale's courageous and far-sighted quest to find a language through which to tell the stories of the Bible in the printed mode for young people in the 1960s is that, by the time his work on *New World* had even begun, it was already ten years too late. By the time he published, a generation had grown up which was witnessing the end of McLuhan's 'Gutenburg Galaxy', the passing of the print-dominated culture and thought forms. Not only had the 1960s cultural revolution ended forever the dominance of the Bible and the hegemony of the Judaeo-Christian culture which had preserved it, but the book culture in which that tradition had been passed on was fast disappearing. This had and continues to have massive implications for the communication of the Christian Gospel which, particularly in the dominant Western Protestant tradition, has been heavily dependent upon the printed word as a vehicle.

Following my sabbatical year in Leicester I returned to Oxford in the autumn of 1979, determined to diversify again in true modular man fashion, by taking over responsibility in the Polytechnic for teaching the Sociology of Education for which I had re-trained. But by this time another generation had emerged which had forgotten the dominance of the written word so favoured still in their schools. Growing up from babyhood with television in their living-rooms and often their bedrooms; encountering stories from the television screen from childhood; frequently encountering new experiences and ideas not from books but from television programming; taking their heroes and role models, their entertainment and their images from television; the children of the eighties were different animals from those with whom I worked with Alan Dale. But like the great man himself, I was equally late in responding to the changes which had taken place. Although it only took me two years in my new role to decide to shift career again and set up the Television Research Unit to look at ways of using the new media of television and video, I was already too late.

I established the unit initially with a small grant from the Joseph Rank Benevolent Trust for a study into the use of television in Sunday School. In its all-too-short history, the TRU conducted major monitoring studies of children's Saturday morning shows for Central Television and then for TVS; a pioneering and influential study of the 1980s rock show *The Tube*; a study of religious radio broadcasts for schools for BBC Radio; an in-depth study of Sunday morning televised worship for BBC Television; a study of lay attitudes to Christian Faith for local radio and the British Council of Churches.[3] At the same time my colleagues and I developed packages using videos of films of classic literature to assist GCSE study, and also found time to become embroiled in controversial Parliamentary legislation to classify home videos. I became involved in my first video production, adapting a Hollywood-made video on child sexual abuse for use in British homes and schools. Our adaptation of Henry Winkler's (the 'Fonz') *Strong Kids Safe Kids* with Sarah Greene, the BBC Children's presenter, was the first to raise public consciousness of this major issue. It also underscored for me the power of video and television usage.

I was not overly interested in theoretical studies of power, control, ownership, ideologies, influence and effects, or the other issues which dominated academic media research groups in the eighties. I had been fascinated by studies into the uses that audiences made of television viewing and into what they had gained from that

---

[3] Published as *Views From The Pews* (British Council of Churches, 1987).

usage. But I was more interested in learning about audiences, and particularly young audiences, and the part that television played in children's and family culture. The projects we undertook consisted largely of acquiring and evaluating masses of data from groups of children in schools nationwide, young people in youth groups, and parents and other adults in churches. We did this through questionnaires on viewing and other cultural habits and through taped discussions of youth and children's programming and religious broadcasts. We incorporated these in regular reports which we submitted to programme makers.

The untreated hard data fed in to producers in these weekly reports may have been superficial and, because of the speed of turnaround required to monitor live shows weekly, the analysis may have been primitive and facile. But my concern was not theoretical but highly practical. I was interested in how television as a medium, and children's programming as a genre, could be used to communicate the story which continued to interest me as an evangelist, the encounter of God and mankind recorded in the Bible.

By the time funding for so elaborate an enterprise as the TRU ran out and further attempts to continue the work in a private company had faltered, I had seen where this was all leading. My illness had forced me to do the hard thinking which led me to seek a way of realising the vision that was dawning in the latter days of the TRU and its spin-offs. The disjointed modular activities in which I had been engaged since arriving in Oxford had given me unique insights, knowledge and training which were waiting to be harnessed. I was privileged to have had these opportunities to diversify, and in 1986 the possibility of taking early retirement from academic life at the age of only 50, with a small lump sum and a small pension, represented the challenge I needed.

My research projects had shown me that Alan Dale's vision had still to be realised. The story was waiting to be told and God had given us a new, challenging medium through which to tell it.

What I should have said to my questioner in Prague is that I thought that maybe God had prepared me, *modular me*, to accept the challenge.

The author with some of his 'charges' in his ministry to pop groups in Manchester in 1965.

Chapter 6

From *Light of the World* to *The Choice*

When the phone call came I thought: 'But I know nothing about animation and I slated the only biblical ones I had reviewed.' The call, my assistant told me, was from John Halas, Hungarian creator of the famous animated version of George Orwell's *Animal Farm*.

With some misgiving, I agreed to meet him. It seemed that his next project was to be a half-hour 'special' for television on the biblical creation story. He wanted my advice. I did not, at that time, even know that a television half-hour is somewhere between 22 and 26 minutes, let alone know enough to advise a great artist in creating a 'special' (whatever that might mean). But apparently it was theological help he wanted.

I had not, up to then, given much thought to cartoon versions of biblical material. I had only taken a serious look at one completed project, the Hanna Barbera biblical series, which Channel 4 asked me to assess for its suitability for broadcast on network television. Commercially at least I got that wrong. I heavily criticised the series conceptually, saying that its seductive format of children time-travelling back to biblical times and participating in the action, trivialised the stories. I advised that the public would reject them. But, as I am frequently reminded by friends in the home-video trade, there are several million reasons why I got it seriously wrong about that series. I had also looked, albeit cursorily, at a very solemn and awesome East European epic. But it was so fiercely religious and reverential that I had not taken it very seriously.

Shortly before John Halas called, I had been briefly intrigued with a notion being promoted in France to create 52 five-minute pieces on the life of Jesus. I flirted for a while with the possibility of becoming involved in it. But, despite the artistic attractiveness of the Japanese shadow-theatre style animation, the script was so conventional and unimaginative, and the voice-over commentator so indelibly 'churchy' – that voice that actors always seem to drop into when reading biblical scripts – that I could not see anyone getting excited. I paid the promoters the courtesy of testing out the pilot five-minute piece both in North America and the UK but, as expected, the broadcasters in North America reacted with polite indifference.

My first meeting with John Halas was very polite but cautious. Hanging over it, like Damocles' sword, was my academic's unease, on the basis of what I had seen up to that point, about the fundamental suitability of the medium in which he excelled for communicating the biblical tradition. John, who was in his late seventies when I met him, was a fine artist and sensitive animator. But he was not a biblical scholar, and he was not as familiar with critical studies of Genesis as he was with Raphael and Michelangelo. The text he wanted to use was the King James, or Authorised Version, and he wanted simply to animate the accounts of the Creation as recorded in the epic form passed on to us by the seventeenth-century translators.

I could see that he was determined to make his 'special' whether I liked it or not; and, because of his eminence in his field, I knew he would succeed. So in a moment of weakness I agreed to act as theological consultant to the project. I persuaded him to reshape the concept by basing it on the notions of Jesus the New Creation as expressed in the Prologue to John's Gospel (John 1:1–14), and of his nativity as the fulfilment of the Old Testament stories. I told myself that my idea was all rather clever and persuaded an Italian broadcaster and TVS, the ITV broadcaster, to part-fund the project.

John got his broadcast. But, in truth, *Light of the World* was a mess conceptually and, as it transpired, artistically. I had broken one of my golden rules, which, in my butterfly career, had always stood me in good stead. I had acted, for once, as the cheerful amateur clergyman who, because he wears a clerical collar, assumes he can turn his hand to anything concerning the Bible. I had arrogantly assumed that, because I had taught Biblical Studies, I could create a concept for a television biblical cartoon. I vowed never to commit that error again. I determined to learn from and with those who knew about animation and to use my experience, knowledge and talents as a biblical scholar and Christian communicator to ensure the academic and educational integrity of the text and content. That meant remembering my mentor Alan Dale's mantra, 'Never be afraid of scholarship', and it meant, instead, using scholarship reverently and skilfully.

I have discovered since moving into this field that it is not only clergy who adopt an arrogant attitude towards the scriptures. Everyone and anyone seems to feel that, because the Bible is in the public domain and freed from copyright restrictions, and because, in the words of a producer at an American network, 'These stories have been around a long time' and the stories are well known, all that is required is some pretty animation, maybe a few assorted animals, some imaginative characters and dialogue and the Bible stories will tell themselves. There are plenty of modern translations of the Bible around, it is argued. There is no need for a working knowledge of the Greek and Hebrew, or even a smattering of the biblical background to the characters or the stories, in order to write them up. The stories are simple. All they need is a little polishing to make them animatable. The attitude seems to be that these stories, old and unprotected by copyright, are fair game for anyone with or without a background understanding of the languages in which they were first written or the message they are meant to convey.

During the ten-year period after I made the decision to tell Bible stories in animation there was a proliferation of biblical animations in Europe and North America; there was then an even greater splurge of attempts to cash in on the success of the format of *The Story Keepers*. These occurred, not only because there is obviously a market for such animations amongst certain sections of the Church-related public, but because it all looks temptingly easy to do: familiar stories; a captive audience addicted to cartoons; reserved slots needing to be filled. It seems to be Christmas come early for anyone with aspirations to be a writer. I have seen scripts of Bible stories from entertainment lawyers, insurance brokers, documentary producers, journalists, Sunday School teachers, housewives, college lecturers, none of whom had any prior knowledge of the biblical texts. I have seen them busy with their Bible open in front of them, blithely rewriting stories of characters they had never previously heard of, and events of cosmic significance of which they had little knowledge and even less understanding, with a breathtaking arrogance which made me cringe and would have made Alan Dale turn in his grave.

A hundred years of biblical scholarship is available. Tomes of dedicated research into biblical language, characters, life and times, history and thought, are to hand. Yet they impiously choose to turn their back on those resources because it is '*only* the Bible' and '*only* a children's cartoon'. I wish I had sometime had the courage to called the bluff of one of the writers. I should have asked the barrister if I could plead in his courtroom because I was an experienced preacher. I should have asked the insurance broker if I could have underwritten a blockbuster movie because I was a trained academic researcher. Or I might have asked the English lecturer if I could give lectures to his students on Dickens or Thomas Hardy because I had lectured on Paul's epistles. After all, I had a smattering of knowledge of those fields, certainly as much as they had in mine when they started to write their biblical stories. To my shame, I never plucked up courage. But I vowed that, for the sake of the integrity of the content I would ensure that, in any production in which I was involved, all translations used would be original and taken from the Greek or Hebrew text, and that all biblical concepts and stories would be carefully approved by scholars of repute and standing in the biblical epistemic communities.

Those of us who are Christians do not need Hollywood to tell us that we are indeed handling the greatest story every told. We know that we have committed to us the sacred task of preserving the story and passing it on to this and future generations. This means that our task is to preserve the integrity of the story. If this in turn means being accused of exclusivity when we object to the sacred stories being handled by those who do not share our commitment to the central Story in them, then so be it. If we have to stand accused of élitism if we insist that only the finest scholars be used to translate and dramatise the stories, then so be that too.

It took me ten years for my translations of biblical stories to reach the screen and for the concept of presenting them in their unique format to be accepted as theologically as well as dramatically suitable. It is galling, if not unexpected, that the success of my academic sweat and labour has not resulted in the acceptance of my emphasis upon the use of scholarship, an acceptance that would be evidenced by the engagement of trained committed biblical scholars in the scripting process of biblical animations. It has led instead to the plagiarising of the format and the concept by the same kind of academically arrogant dilettantes that I had to face down as soon as I began to seek support for my vision.

Taking the risk by being awkward and sticking to that principle has proved personally satisfying, and it has been good to win the plaudits of one's peers. Professor Chris Rowlands put a generally held view when he wrote of *The Story Keepers* in the *Times Educational Supplement*:

> It seems to me, as somebody who has spent his life looking at Biblical Studies, that it is an effective way of getting the message

across, and one which has taken account of the way the stories might have been used in the first century. So there's quite a nod in the direction of 100 years of biblical scholarship.[1]

A television critic, David Bridge, comparing *The Story Keepers* with a rival American production, wrote:

> [The one] treats the Bible purely as a book of fantastic stories and sets it in the context of a narrative involving fantastic . . . cartoon characters. The message is clear: the Bible has as much to do with real life as Tom and Jerry and Mickey Mouse. *The Story Keepers* on the other hand, though it also uses a cartoon format, has a really interesting story line and makes it clear that the stories of Jesus are the stories of a real person. Its message is that to be a follower of Jesus requires courage and a sense of humour and it would be hard to improve on that.[2]

Despite this praise, however, I am not convinced from what I am beginning to see around me that the fight for the principle has been successful. As a producer sympathetically remarked, when he saw yet another of the semi-plagiaristic copies of my work on television: 'I don't suppose you can copyright your approach, can you?'

It is only human, I suppose, that seeing another un-academic biblical animation by another biblically untrained uncommitted writer, that I feel disappointment and frustration. But in my higher moments I content myself with saying that the fight was worth it and remains so. After all, it is another attempt to tell stories which the biblically illiterate have never previously heard. I must be thankful for the smallest of mercies.

John Halas had movingly revealed that he had one great ambition left. He wanted to create a life of Christ in animation.

---

[1] Prof. Christopher Rowlands quoted in 'The Gospel According to Brian', *Times Educational Supplement Friday Magazine*, 16 October 1998.
[2] David Bridge, *Methodist Recorder*, 10 January 2000.

That was the final impetus I needed. In late 1987 I persuaded the BBC to part-fund a development project and I decided to test the water. If I succeeded in raising the main bulk of the funding, the BBC under Michael Grade agreed to co-produce. The first task was to gather my academic advisers, and I began the work, which has gone on ever since, of visiting other theologians, scholars, church leaders, teachers, seeking their support for my enterprise. I went not only to try to enthuse them for the possibilities of using animation as a medium for retelling the stories of the Bible, but also to listen to their comments and seek their advice. During 1988 I had gathered my resource group of advisers: three professors of theology, an Anglican priest-cum-BBC producer, a Catholic religious, a Methodist biblical scholar, a Dutch theologian and a rabbi.

The second task was to develop a format, a style, an approach, which was not only interesting as television but academically acceptable. By 12 February 1989, as a result of 18 months of consultations and meetings, the core of what was eventually to emerge as the 'story-within-a-story', the 'story wrap-around' 'the contextual approach' format, of *The Story Keepers*, had been established. I smile when I am asked where this distinctive and commercially attractive format came from. For although I made important modifications in the ensuing years as a result of continuing discussions in the UK, Ireland and the USA, the core of the format remained the same as it was in the BBC-funded project of 1988–90. It is laid out in a memorandum I circulated to my advisers on that date, 12 February 1989, for our meeting the following week. Re-reading it after almost 11 years it still sounds fresh. According to the memorandum:

> The thrust of the presentation is that the stories were first preserved and circulated in oral form, repeated at informal and more formal meetings of Christians and retold to respond to or provoked by certain situations. The series focuses on groups of Christians meeting in Rome in homes and secret places during

the persecutions in the weeks prior to the death of Peter which may have prompted the writing down of the stories.[3]

The last sentence was modified at the meeting to be '*following* the death of Peter'. Two storylines were to run parallel: firstly, the story-telling community during a period of severe persecution, with their fear, courage, and motivation for preserving and telling the story; and secondly, the stories they told about Jesus and remembered of what he said, all placed contextually in first-century Rome and Palestine in the days of Jesus. The paper goes on to say that the basic text used is Mark's gospel:

> Only those parts of Lukan and Matthaen material which cannot be left out and would be expected in a television presentation are included. Similarly only those parts of John are included which cannot be omitted . . . as far as possible the scripts try not to mix traditions in one episode. The texts also stress both the political and social situation in which the stories were preserved and told, and that against which the stories took place.

In front of me, and constantly brought to the attention of the advisers, was Alan Dale's *New World* and the workbook I published to go with it in 1970, *The Choice*. Chapter 5 of the workbook is entitled 'The sign of the fish' and talks of the secret meetings of Christians held behind closed doors in Nero's Rome following the first persecutions. The clandestine meeting places, the chapter tells the young readers, were known to Christians by the *ichthus* sign chalked on the doors.[4] Once inside, the Christians told each other stories of Jesus, passing them on orally because they had not yet been written down.

---

[3] Memorandum to Advisers, 12 February 1989.

[4] 'On the door of the house they chalked their secret sign . . . the sign of a fish. The last to arrive wiped off the chalk, to keep the meeting secret. The sign comes from the Greek word for fish, *ichthus*. The letters of the word are the first letters of the Greek for "Jesus Christ, Son of God,

It was this concept which underlay the voice-over for the pilot which John Halas produced in 1990. It is also the concept which underlay the voice-over for a promotional video, *The Story*, produced in 1993 by Don Bluth, and the voice-over for the opening 90-second introduction which precedes each episode of *The Story Keepers*. In the same way, episode 1 of *Story Keepers* is an expansion of the pilot John Halas made in 1990.[5] The similarity between the three is tribute to the work of the advisers in 1989. The uniqueness of the concept belongs to them.

In April 1994 I was driving from Los Angeles through the San Fernando valley with the writer, David Weiss. He had just been recruited to head up the writing team for the Irish–American series which was to be based on the BBC concept and which became *The Story Keepers*. At that time he had only the vaguest notion of what the concept was. Indeed, he was under the impression that he had to devise a concept from scratch. However, by the time we reached Ventura I had told him our ideas and enthused him with the power of the concept and the format which had been developed. Within a day, after an exciting brain thrash with two other Americans, we had outlined episode 1 of *The Story Keepers*. Within a further two exhausting days we had outlined the next two episodes. Again, this was only possible because of the work of the advisers five years before, and their commitment to scholarship. Fortunately, David Weiss was astute enough to recognise that as well. On my return he wrote to me:[6] 'I was quite pleased with the outcome of our meeting and look forward to commencing the minor revisions on *The Story* as soon as your funding is in place . . . Major elements from the original

---

[4] (*continued*)   your Saviour". If you go to Rome, it is claimed that you can still see the secret sign scratched on the walls of the catacombs by the Christians in those terrible years.' Brian Brown, *The Choice* (Denholm House/E. J. Arnold, 1970), pp. 48–53.

[5] See appendix.

[6] David Weiss, letter to Brian Brown, 25 April 1994.

script (draft 2) that *will not* be changed shall include the following . . .' He then goes on to list the characters who 'keep the story of Jesus alive via the oral tradition . . . [they] will use the circumstances of their everyday adventures as a starting point from which to tell their stories of Christ's life and teaching'.

It had taken five years since I produced the memorandum to the BBC advisers for that original concept to be turned into a script. 'It is an exciting and worthwhile project,' wrote David Weiss. He and his fellow writers were to make it reality in the coming 15 months.

The author with The Merseybeats, 1965.

Chapter 7

My parish or my oyster

The familiar bright eyes sparkled as he rose to greet me. He was ten years older than when we first met in 1989. But the greeting was just as warm: 'Brian. You made it! Congratulations! After all your struggles you made it. I knew you would from the first time I met you. You were totally committed and determined.' We were meeting at a hotel in Los Angeles where he was attending a board meeting of the National Interfaith Cable Coalition and I had meetings with its President.

He was right. My vision and I had come a long way since that late afternoon at Kennedy airport in New York when I had come looking for him in the lounge. It had been my first visit to North America. I knew no one.

'Look for a big guy with a black bushy beard,' he had told me. He was not difficult to spot. Roy Lloyd was, and still is, media consultant to the National Council of Churches in the USA. I was told that he knows everyone there is to know in media. I saw over time how true that was.

Having created the concept and the format, with some funding from the Welsh broadcaster S4C, the BBC and a bank loan, I had commissioned John Halas to make a pilot. He did so with a Welsh production company. On the basis of the concept and the pilot, the BBC the agreed to co-produce and part-fund the production of 52 five-minute programmes. Now all I had to do was raise the £3 million I would need to finance the production of the series. The financiers had said that I had to have American pre-sales or investment so, in my usual nothing-to-be-lost-everything-to-be-gained way, I landed in New York to meet the man who knew everyone and who was to introduce me around.

Thus began a series of journeys and meetings, firstly in New York at the National Council of Churches and the American Bible Society, and with individuals like Roy Lloyd; then, through Roy's introduction, at Turner Broadcasting in Atlanta. This was followed by further exhausting, rapid-fire trips and meetings with broadcasters, theologians and church leaders in the USA and all over Europe. Certainly great enthusiasm was aroused, long-lasting friendships established and experiences shared, notably with several Roman Catholic bishops across Europe, and with Archbishop John Foley, Secretary of the Papal Council for Social Communication in whose office close to the Papal apartments he and I prayed. I was reminded of these flying visits after I lectured to the EBU Conference in Prague in 1999 when a woman I recognised approached. 'The Archbishop sends his greetings,' she said. It was his personal secretary who had come to hear me speak ten years after my visit to the Vatican.

By the end of three years, however, I had many new friends, a huge overdraft and mounting debts, but no funding for my vision. The pilot was generally rejected as not sufficiently appealing or arresting. Although everyone said the general concept of a story-telling community retelling stories of Jesus was exciting, the final outcome did not live up to the expectations. Worse than these criticisms, however, was the fact that I was no nearer raising the finance in 1991 than I had been four years earlier. The debts by now were too big even to be sensibly worrying. We had set up a small company and had an overdraft facility with a major high-street bank secured against our house, which we had already remortgaged twice in order to fund the development.

The period in which I chose to start fund-raising was not the most economically auspicious, to put it mildly. The recession of the late 1980s was deepening on the money markets. Bank rate and interest rates were at historically high levels. The banks were charging upwards of 18 per cent for overdrafts and loan facilities. Banks and finance companies were collapsing both in the UK and in the USA.

The shake-out of accountants and bank personnel in the City following the 'Big Bang', the insurance scandals, the company failures and tight money led to the emergence of a proliferation of self-styled consultants and finance advisers looking to use their skills and experience – particularly in fund-raising for potentially lucrative television projects. Unfortunately for me, they all seemed to make a beeline for me and my project which they saw as a potential gold-mine. There was the ex-banker and his former assistant who set up as film finance advisers and to whom I was introduced not long after I started the project. He wanted an up-front, non-returnable fee of £15,000 (which he reduced to £10,000 because he said he had a personal interest in the project) in return for introducing me to a sympathetic bank which might, only *might*, offer to finance the project. Then there was the insurance broker who talked of financing the project against a new bond he was developing; and the French lawyer who, taking benefit of new tax-shelter laws in Luxembourg, supposedly meant to encourage the development of the film and television production industry in the Duchy, offered to put up 40 per cent of the budget to add to the 12.5 per cent the BBC were offering to contribute. He was followed by an executive of the profligate British and Commonwealth Bank who offered to bankroll the project without any security or pre-sale agreements, at high rates of interest. My hopes were high as my wife and I travelled back from a short holiday during the Spring bank holiday week in 1990. Unfortunately, on the journey I heard that receivers had been called in only hours before our loan application came before the bank's Credit Committee for final approval.

Then there was the European subsidiary of a large American bank which, the following day, agreed to replace the failed

British bank as the funding bank for the series. The offer was approved by the parent bank within two weeks and long, lawyer-expensive hours were clocked up as the so-called due diligences were conducted on the project (meaning that the bank were checking every detail of every contract and forecast in order to satisfy themselves that, although they would take a huge 18 per cent interest from the transaction, they would have no risk). Before the negotiations commenced a large facility fee was exacted and when, barely months later, the US parent bank, without warning, closed down their London operation, we were left to pay the bank's legal bill for a top City commercial law practice. This, even when it was halved, still left us with an account for £16,000 to meet and my wife having to forfeit her redundancy lump sum to meet it.

Then there was the 'born-again Christian' finance adviser who, for a non-returnable fee of £50,000, would use his good offices to raise the finance, without, of course, any guarantees. And the other finance adviser who introduced me to a French bank and demanded a success fee of 8 per cent of what the bank loaned. Even one of the bank management tried to get in on the act, introducing me to one of the bank's wealthy Christian customers, in return for the usual 'consideration' of course. By the time I had been introduced to an American financier with access to money in Swiss, Bahamian and Cayman Island accounts, and to the 'wealthy Channel Islander' who drove around London in a hired Rolls conducting his business from the back seat, I had travelled countless miles and met all kinds of people and tried all sorts of sources of revenue, for no return whatsoever.

I was then introduced to what I was told by a film insurance broker were two Irish bankers. They turned out to be a former film accountant and her partner. They said that they had access to money, via the Irish film tax shelter. By this time I was growing weary of the constant round of presentations, and with the bank becoming extremely restless for repayment of the overdraft, I was prepared to listen to anybody. They sounded no less plausible than the other potential finance providers. They told me they had a pool of investors in Ireland who wished to take advantage of Section 35 new Irish tax laws whereby companies investing upwards of IR£1.1 million in film or television projects could write off 40 per cent against corporation tax.

The condition for the investment was that a maximum of 60 per cent of the budget could be covered, provided that a minimum of 75 per cent of the budget was spent in Ireland by the employment of Irish tax-paying personnel. Although this effectively would put paid to the BBC's involvement as 12.5 per cent co-producers, I had no other viable option. Nothing ventured nothing gained, I flew in to meet the studio through which the investment would be passed.

I was aware that the project would have to be made in Ireland by an Irish studio and that, in order for the producing company to take advantage of the Section 35 investment opportunities and the other tax benefits available, I would have to assign the rights over to the company. Those more experienced in film and television production have subsequently warned me about the folly of assigning away rights. But I always reply that my lawyer, a specialist in intellectual property rights, did warn me; but like me, he realised I had little option. Unlike all those to whom I went for finance, I was not interested in making a personal profit. Above all, I was not looking for long-term income. On the contrary, we both knew that I had only two motivations. I had run all over Europe and the United States because I had a vision I wanted to realise: I wanted to make the series for Paddy and his peers. I also had a massive bank debt and my home was at risk. I would grab at any opportunity to make the series and to clear the debts.

When, later, I was again faced with the decision about assigning the rights, I was in the same situation. If I wanted to raise money via the tax shelter to make my series and to repay my debts, I would have to have the film made by an Irish company in an Irish studio. To raise any money, that company had to own the rights. I had no option but to assign them over.

I was shocked to discover, on arrival in the centre of Dublin's new media and arts district, that the studio to which I was recommended was in grave financial trouble, despite having received heavy government subsidies. It was about to go into receivership owing thousands to the revenue commissioners. Fortunately, although they tried hard in the couple of weeks I was with them to persuade me to assign my rights to their company, I did not do so. I realised that this was another blind alley and broke off dealings before it was too late. I learned later that they had been telling their creditors that they had acquired a valuable new asset which would turn their fortunes around. Some months later I heard that in another part of Dublin an animated Bible series was being made by a company calling itself by the title of my book, *The Choice*. Even more oddly, the first episode bore the same title as Chapter 5 in the book. I wondered where that idea had come from.

The two-pronged imperative – to make the series and to clear the debts – which drove me to Ireland in the first place, hung over me throughout the next five stressful years as I commuted to and worked in Dublin. The problem with being so driven is that, in the burning zeal to achieve the good and worthy goal, the end may not necessarily justify the means. It can certainly distort moral certainties and lead to compromises which, under less-driven circumstances, would never have been countenanced. I am a minister and an academic, not an accountant, a commercial lawyer or a businessman. I am less used to the world of greys, of turning the blind eye 'because it is business', where different rules are deemed to apply.

I am also English and not Irish. Except for one holiday in the 1960s I had never met Irish people except in England under English conditions, under British rules. That in itself created its own problems because I quickly realised that I was not just a stranger in Dublin 2, but I was a foreigner. I was an outsider in what the Dubliners acknowledge is a tight-knit, village-like community with its own rituals, rules and way of working, its own hierarchies and power structures, its own hidden meanings. In such a community power is exercised by the nod and the whisper. I did not know the rules. I was not part of the structure.

Fortunately, I was part of the worldwide Methodist family and from my first days in the foreign capital I was taken under the wing of my fellow Methodist ministers and their people. They offered me hospitality in their homes, and when it became evident that I would need to stay for lengthy periods in central Dublin, I was also given free meals and a room in a church hostel run by the Central Methodist Church. My wife and I will always be grateful to the Dublin Methodists for their generosity. Although other individual Christian friends have been generous to a fault, the minister and members of Dublin Central Methodist Church are the only church group who have given us anything since we started. And they did not wait for us to ask.

I was also part of the ecumenical church and was warmly welcomed by my fellow clergy, particularly those in the three other dominant traditions, the Roman Catholics, the Church of Ireland and the Presbyterians. The fellowship of the church was all the more appreciated because the struggle to raise the money, and later to cashflow the productions, took me into situations for which, from my sheltered Oxford background, I was quite unprepared. The escape to the Methodist church hostel at the end of a day of unease was therapeutic.

I was prepared to compromise my conscience because of the overriding vision. It would be worth it for 'Liverpool Paddy', I told myself, at times not over-convincingly. At first it seemed innocent enough in the wider scheme of things: the whispered 'You're an artist if anyone asks you' as a government voucher for a free flight to Heathrow was slipped into my hand; an accountant suggesting that I could avoid tax by claiming residence as a writer in the Republic. But as the project developed and the financing started to come together, the compromises for the sake of the vision became more worrying. I told myself I was not familiar with the workings of business and I watched bemused as the studio which had invited me over collapsed. I was quite unprepared for the whisperings and abusive phone calls demanding compensation from members of the staff whom I had met only briefly, and who were singling me out as a likely source of lay-off money.

I was still shell-shocked from that experience when gradually a group of businessmen began to emerge who this time seemed genuinely interested, and not just in using me and my project for thr own ends. They seemed to offer a genuine possibility that my twin goals would be achieved. When they agreed to start up the company by making a pilot and by investing risk money, fear of losing them had become uppermost in my mind and it seemed churlish for me to refuse their demand that I assign the rights. On my lawyer's advice I insisted that the assignment would be dependent upon a payment by the company of the £100,000 to clear the overdraft of the company we had set up to develop the concept. I duly agreed to take shares in the company and signed the shareholders' agreement.

The pilot which emerged contained only three minutes of animation, some stills and a voice-over. But it was high quality. It was far more interesting than the earlier pilot for the BBC and so was the screenplay, which by then I had written in longhand into two drafts of 52 five-minute programmes. A chance encounter with an American publisher in London led to me talking to his colleagues at their publishing house, and then to my making a major presentation to an impressive array of top executives in Hollywood. Negotiations commenced which resulted in the signing of a major pre-sale contract for television and video exploitation in North America. We had what everyone for six years had been telling me was necessary. North America was 70 per cent of the market, they said. You need an American deal.

I could not believe how well things had turned out. The North American sale would cover the 60 per cent of the budget the tax beneficial investors were making available and which had to be covered before they would release their cash. The contract with the Americans included a declaration that the project was fully funded and would be backed by an insurance completion bond guaranteeing that the series would be delivered to time and to the agreed budget. I decided not to ask where the other 40 per cent was coming from and not to ask to see the completion bond. That might have produced embarrassing answers I was in no mood to hear. I had what I had been working six years for. I was going to get my series. That was all that mattered.

When I was given two contracts to sign which promised me the £100,000 for the rights and fees for my services as series executive producer and writer, cashflowed in complicated tranches, my lawyer insisted that specific dates be given upon which the payments would be made. I was told, in no uncertain terms, that no such specific dates could or would be given, and unless I signed then and there the project could not go ahead. I could not risk failure after all the waiting, so I agreed. But my lawyer won a concession. A stop date, beyond which payment would not be deferred was inserted.

I also demurred when, at the last minute, my contract as series executive producer which, as is standard practice, gave me overall responsibility for bringing the production in and final say in all matters, was substantially amended by the repeated insertion of the circumscribing phrase 'with the producer' whenever my responsibilities were laid out. I was effectively neutered from the start. However, I was a foreigner, I was not a businessman and I wanted nothing to stand in the way of the series being made. I would agree to anything to ensure it was.

The first nine months of production were bizarre. The company had commissioned a major Dublin studio to produce the series and it was made abundantly clear that I, the stranger with the clerical collar, was not over-welcome in the studio, despite my title and my contract. A Spanish director was appointed, but I noticed that he was absent more than he was there. I had limited previous experience of creating a children's animation, but the appointed producer, a free-lance accountant who had been instrumental in raising the finance, had less than I: he had none whatsoever. He had decided to leave the day-to-day production to the studio. I kept my counsel and concentrated on working with the scripting team to adapt the scripts I brought for children's half-hour shows.

I was, however, in the front line as the production company's representative – their *virtual face* on the Point Team, which was set up to superintend the scripting process.[1] Members of the Point Team expressed concern that every time the Head Writer or individual members of the Point Team rang to speak to the director he was not available. I can still recall the discomfort I felt when I was asked about this. I knew that the director was working in Spain and in America, not on our project, although he was supposedly on the payroll. But for the sake of the project I joined the cover-up and said nothing. My face was red with embarrassment as I helped compose *aide-mémoires* of meetings of the Point Team through the winter and spring of 1994–5. These called for a face-to-face meeting with the director so that the Point Team could repeat directly to him their frequent calls of dissatisfaction with his work. I could hardly disagree, and I supported the *aides-mémoires* with several concerned memos of my own, warning of the unhappiness of the Americans.

As I now re-read the voluminous notes and memoranda I submitted to the studio and my production colleagues, I clearly was almost at the end of my patience with a situation I was not used to. In May 1995 one of my American colleagues, knowing my frustration, faxed me to say: 'Hang in there, friend: you are absolutely essential to this wonderful, but sometimes crazy process for this timeless project. Remember, we'll tell our great-

---

[1] Point Team is an American term adapted from Point Person, the individual to whom and through whom everything in a project has to pass. The Point Team as a body, which included representatives from Zondervan and Focus on the Family, as well as David Weiss, the Head Writer, and myself, performed this role in relation to the scripts and content of *The Story Keepers*.

great-grandchildren 'bout these crazy days someday as they watch Ben & Helena on their holographic laser.' So I bit my tongue and soldiered on, even when the Point Team made a scheduled visit to Dublin to look at the studio and were greeted by a large team of experienced animators in the studios, several of whom, as at least one of the Point Team besides me knew, had been drafted in specially for the day to replace the young inexperienced crew and students who had occupied the building the previous day.

Within months the production studio which we had engaged in good faith and trust, ran out of money and went bankrupt. By this time they had produced just three substandard episodes which, as I had warned in memo after memo, the Americans rejected. The production studio bosses had been paid half of their costs upfront and this money went with them when they collapsed.

We had planned to launch the series at a book fair in America, but this now had to be cancelled. I none the less went along on my own to face the ire and the disappointment of the Americans. They, however, knew I had been continually expressing my concerns, and they knew that, from the beginning, any responsibility for the final product had been taken from me by the studio.

An experienced supervising director was taken on who performed minor miracles in turning the disastrous performance of his predecessors around. He and the supervising producer, whom he and I recommended to take over leadership of a new studio team, are alone responsible for bringing in the series. Unfortunately, the only economic way they could do so was by shipping the animation to a studio in Korea. As the voice recordings had been done in Charlotte, North Carolina, I did my writing in the UK, David Weiss and the script team were in California, and the music was composed and recorded in Germany, the production was largely being created outside the Republic. This was troublesome because not only had the company undertaken to employ a large number of Irish passport holders but, as I understood it, it was a condition of the tax beneficial investment that 75 per cent of the production would be done in the Republic.

The decision to reorganise in this way was a correct business decision. It ensured that the series was delivered. I was bothered that if it was not illegal (and I am not a lawyer or closely familiar with the Irish tax laws) the reorganised way of working was ethically disturbing. But I told myself that this was a business decision and I was not a businessman. As long as it resulted in the completion of my series, I should be satisfied.

In 1997, less than two years later, after much pressured work the final episode arrived from Korea and was mixed with the voiceover from Charlotte, using the scripts from Oxford and Los Angeles and the music from Munich. All I could do was to admire the *chutzpah*, and be thankful that the supervising director had performed his minor miracles and we had delivered. That we were over a year behind schedule and had not called upon a completion bond was another miracle. I did not receive the money I was due during production or by the final cut-off date in the contracts. This did not entirely surprise me, although I never really understood why payment had to take so long. I had to wait a further three years even to receive a portion as settlement. But I had achieved my vision. Even if my family and I had to bear the cost of it.

In December 1999 the Chief Executive of an American Network Company wrote to me: 'I'm delighted you have persevered with *The Story Keepers* because, as you recall, it has long been a favourite program idea of mine.' And I think, looking back: if she only knew . . .

The frustrating part of the long trail through the mire of dubious financial deals, and learning and losing the hard way as I went, is that those years of travel and scrabbling after finance led me to take my eye off the ball. I realise, looking back, that I would have been more usefully employed, and my time more profitably spent, if I had concentrated on getting the concept and the format right. The cool reception to the John Halas pilot should have told me that, even had I been successful in my financial quest before I went to Ireland, the final product could well have not been right.

Chapter 8

The Promised Land

At Easter 1995, at the height of one of the most stressful periods in the production, a group of us met in my home church in Oxford to celebrate the Jewish Festival of Pesach, in which Jews recall the rescue of the people of Israel in the great exodus under Moses. In times of distress and pain in succeeding centuries this annual reminder of God's saving act has inspired Jewish people with hope. For, as they endured the pain and indignity of slavery in Egypt, the Jews must have despaired time and again, and wondered when the suffering would end and they would see signs of hope. The prophet Moses gave them that hope, and under his leadership they began the journey which led them to the Promised Land. The scriptures tell us that there were times on the journey when they gave up hope of ever getting there. There were times when even the slavery they had endured before was more bearable than the pain they had to endure in the desert.

My own journey since I set out to fulfil my vision had frequently been painful, and was to become more so before I reached the end. In 1996, a year before the series was completed, I was hurried back into the John Radcliffe Hospital in Oxford for four more cardiac operations to repair the four coronary artery grafts I had received in 1983. At that point I thought I might never see the realisation of my dream. I thought that perhaps, like Moses, I would only glimpse the Promised Land, and that others would complete the journey I had started. My faith, burning low, was restored by continual reminders of the faith and hope of the Jewish people, which sustained them then and has done ever since, even during the worst of persecution. All that I and they have in common is hope and a vision which inspired that hope. Mine was fulfilled two months after my final operation.

On 12 January 1997 ITV launched the series on UK network terrestrial television with a 90-second introduction, based on the two pilots made in 1990 and 1993, setting the scene for what was to follow. The series, finally entitled *The Story Keepers*, broke all viewing records for children's religious broadcasting, and broke new ground in religious broadcasting generally. Many British broadcasters and critics hailed it as a broadcasting phenomenon. It was soon transmitted a second time; a compilation special was shown; and further re-runs began in January 2000.

Critics recognised that, although the series was overtly religious in content and made no attempt to hide or water down the three or more gospel stories in each episode, it nonetheless achieved something unique by dint of high quality animation and high production values; humorous and exciting scripting; careful, unabashed use of biblical and historical scholarship; and close attention to rationale, concept and format.

Its blend of entertainment and sacred story, excitement and commitment, adventure and belief resulted in high ratings and audiences from all ages, all walks of life, from within and outside faith communities.

Since that time, as the originator and the one associated with the series for the longest period of time, I seem to have written and talked most about the theories and concepts underlying it.[1]

---

[1] Brian Brown, 'A Vision Becomes Reality', taped lecture given at the National Christian Resources Exhibition, Sandown Park, 1992; 'Right at Last: Keeping the Gospel Stories Alive', *Viewpoints* (March 1977), pp. 5–8; 'Not Being Afraid of Scholarship', *Connect* (Spring 1998), p. 13. These short articles give necessarily less complete accounts of the issues and events related in this book.

The success story of *The Story Keepers*

- 29 per cent audience share on ITV network in the UK

- watched by 49 per cent of 4–9 year olds watching TV at the time

- 1.4 million viewers

- outscoring all other children's programming from terrestrial, cable and satellite

- screened on Sundays at peak viewing time for children

- screened at a time when church-going children not watching

Amid all the talking there comes one recurring question asked by journalists, researchers, academics and broadcasting professionals: 'Where did you get the idea from?' Or, 'Where did the concept and the format arise from?' As one US network interviewer pleaded, after being exasperated by my academically trained, garrulous inability to give the short, pithy, all-embracing snap answer he was looking for: 'Give me a sound bite. All I want is a sound bite!' How could I tell him my convoluted personal history in a sound bite?

This obsession with discovering the simple, single genesis of new ideas is one of the paradoxes of the increasingly complex intellectual universe we inhabit. We are almost pre-Copernican in our search for one originator, one source, one *prima causa* of new ideas. We do not seem able to cope with the notion of the evolution over time of new approaches – even to the development of a concept for a television series – involving a multitude of creative minds, requiring patient self-criticism and a long process of dissatisfied listening, reading, discussion, critiques, evaluation, more reading and reordering. But that is how the *Story Keepers* phenomenon evolved.

Perhaps in our strange media world where intellectual properties are bought and sold, where agents and contract lawyers fight on behalf of clients to preserve ownership and seek the highest financial reward for their clients, original creativity is a commodity to be guarded with the kind of secrecy which those of us from the world of academia find hard to understand or live by. As a former academic, I am used to openness, to sharing my ideas and listening to and adapting those of my peers. I have always sought both to discuss my ideas freely and to seek advice and criticism from fellow academics and other people with ideas.

Since I changed course and left my cosy career as a teacher and researcher in the dreaming spires of Oxford, I have horrified colleagues, media lawyers and agents because of my openness to discuss my ideas in public and in publications, and my willingness to embrace and act upon criticisms or suggestions made by others.

'You can't tell them that. They'll use it,' they constantly warn. 'You can't take up his suggestion. He'll want credit and payment.' As proof of the folly of my naïveté in releasing such precious material so openly, they point to the fact that there was a video in circulation three months before the first episode of *The Story Keepers* was delivered let alone published. It contained three episodes based upon various papers and drafts of scripts and translations that I had been circulating for comment for over three years before I first arrived in Ireland.

It is ironic that in the days not long after I had completed the first longhand draft of *The Story*, upon which *The Story Keepers* was based, an article appeared in one of the broadsheets alleging that the originator of *Postman Pat* received few rewards from the burgeoning business exploiting the character he had created. When I agreed to assign the rights away the warning of 'another Postman Pat' rang in my ears. I know now what the article meant.

In my more jaundiced moments, as I see not only that ideas and concepts over which I sweated for years are being exploited by others, but that numerous claims of varying degrees of dubiousness have been made to ownership of the ideas I was openly discussing, I am forced to ask whether, maybe, the media lawyers have been proved right. Perhaps they have, and this is the price I must pay for my liberal approach to the sacredness of intellectual property rights. Perhaps they are right in saying that, in a greedy world, missionary vision is not compatible with the harsh realities of business.

I have had to learn that in the grey world of origins, the slightest claim is the lawyer's pay cheque. Because we are obsessed with possession and reward, it seems we need to stake our claim for sole ownership of ideas. It is so much cleaner for lawyers, agents and bankers if the origins of ideas, and therefore ownership of the rights to them, can apparently be traced to one single person and one blinding moment of inspiratn. It is so much easier to be able to say: 'That was all mine. I conceived that idea.' That is all very attractive to the rights purchasers, but somewhat unrealistic to those who devise the formats and draft the scripts. It is far removed from the real world of drafts, redrafts, discussion, criticism, crossing out, tearing up, total rewrites, in which those of us who do the actual creating live. It is even further from the world of evangelical mission with no thought of personal gain.

The evolution of the concept, rationale and format of *The Story Keepers* was agonizingly slow, painful and arduous. It took almost eight years of struggle to get it anywhere near right. It took thousands of miles of travel, visiting church leaders and theologians of all traditions in Europe and North America – from the Pope's media adviser in the Vatican to Southern Baptist publishers in the Bible Belt – seeking to persuade them that the enterprise was not only viable but a justified use of a Methodist minister's time and effort. It took hours of conversations with animators and writers. Above all it took years of face-to-face meetings with broadcasters, particularly schedulers, and video- and book-distributors to convince them that there was an audience for the series, and that that potential market justified their advancing the almost $6 million it eventually took to create and produce the series.

There were times when even I, with my almost obsessional determination to tear up and start again in order it get it right, nearly faltered. As the Bank pressed and the house was remortgaged again, to keep our head above water and the dream alive, even I wondered whether it would ever see the light of day. But when those first 90 seconds appeared on screen my gratitude was not that we had a success and that my faith was vindicated, but that the concept was at last seen to be right. But it took longer than a sound bite to get it so.

Looking back, I can see no one conversation during those eight or so years' gestation which had that 'Ah that's it!' flash that changed everything. I can single out no one individual, no one book, no one research paper, no one evaluation, which stands out as more distinctive than any other.

As for myself, I cannot claim originality in any particular field. If I have any quality, it is doggedness, an almost bloody-minded tenacity and an inability to recognise when I am beaten. I am not a ground-breaking theologian. I am no great Greek or Hebrew scholar, although I stuck to my tenet that all the translations and dramatisations used in *The Story Keepers* and my follow-on work would be my own original translations from the original texts direct into animation, and not derived from second-hand translations published by the great religious publishing houses. I am not an original literary thinker. I am principally a teacher. I listen. I absorb what others in their ivory towers write and say, and I pass it on. I make what I learn accessible, particularly to the young.

If I had any central role in the creation of the distinctive *Story Keepers* rationale and format, it was as the synthesiser, the listener and adapter who brought all together to make the concept and format what they were evolving to be. As a radio producer once put it to me: 'It always needs someone to do the lateral thinking to bring the diverging strands together into a coherent rationale.'

Not all those involved in the production may have understood the rationale as it evolved, nor grasped the significance of the various changes in direction. Not all necessarily understood why I chose one particular biblical passage at a particular point, or why I suggested a certain character should have certain characteristics. Nor did the writers or the animators necessarily understand why I wanted a certain style used. But whether they did or not was almost irrelevant. It was their and my strict adherence to the rationale which was evolving which made possible the story-within-story-within-story format, which is so apparently simple and so attractive that people now ask: 'Why did no one think of it before?'.

Chapter 9

From concept to script

Although the essence of the concept, rationale and format was laid down in the group meetings of advisers at the BBC, the scripts which finally emerged for *The Story Keepers* are radically different from the first hesitant drafts kicked around in 1989–90. In genesis language, they are a result of long evolution, not of a Big Bang. They began as five-minute re-tellings of Bible stories, with no attention to context, backstory or character development. Over ten years, however, they developed into 26-minute animated dramas set in real historical situations, focusing on real and imaginative characters living out created faction adventures, in which they tell biblical stories in fast-moving contexts of danger and excitement. What began with the intention to inform and educate young minds about the content of gospel stories, was transformed through the creative evolution of the concept into entertaining, gripping adventures of real heroes preserving and passing on life-affirming stories in life-threatening situations.

The process, however, was not ordered and controlled. Rather, it was haphazard and stumbling. An American partner called it 'divine serendipity'; another friend parodied it as 'Brian's stupidity'. Mixing the genesis metaphors, it was chaos theory rather than creation *ex nihilo*! But it was the process of lateral thinking after a series of apparently contradictory ideas had come together, standing back and making the theory fit the praxis in classic sociological fashion, which crystallised the rationale and the format.

The one consistent factor was my dissatisfaction with the two models which were available to me when I began in 1988. I had long been a critic, in my academic days, of what I term the 'recontextual model' of biblical animations favoured by at least three of the 'successful' biblical animation series currently available on the North American Christian market. By this model, an imaginary fantasy situation is created as the 'MacGuffin', the creative trick, to lead in to the Bible story.[1] A group of kids play around on an archaeological dig; they fall down a hole; they walk along a passage; they step through a golden door and find themselves back in biblical times and they re-enact a biblical adventure. That model made me distinctly uneasy. Whether the trick was time travel in a spaceship, or imaginative trips of fantasy via a computer cursor, I argued that if the only way contemporary children can enter the biblical experience is through fantasy and flights of imagination, then we should not be surprised if, for the young viewer, the biblical stories themselves are relegated to the world of fantasy and imagination. That, of course, is fine if you see the stories as fantasy or artefacts created by human imagination. But what if the biblical stories really are significant, life-affirming vehicles of truths about humanity and our relationship with God? Are we not misusing the medium if, by its use, we distort the central truths of the stories we are seeking to communicate?

I knew it was this mode which academics had in mind when, every time I talked about making the Bible available to children through animation, they asked the $64,000 question. I used to remind them of the work of Alan Dale in the mid 1960s, producing the first written translation of the Old and New Testaments

---

[1] 'MacGuffin' is a term coined by Alfred Hitchcock for the twist or trick in his mystery films, and now generally used by writers for the trick or twist in the format or plot.

in graded language accessible to, and understandable by, children with reading ages of 9 to 13. I would go on to say that my own research had shown that 20 years later, for the majority of children, television had replaced the book as the primary medium through which they encountered new knowledge. Now, I would triumphantly proclaim, we must use television and, because all my research indicated further that the cartoon was the most popular form of television for children, we must use animation. The response I would get was, and by some still is: 'How do you tell real stories about real people, set in real historical time and place, which have had profound effects upon the history and culture and beliefs of Western society, in a medium more appropriate for the world of fantasy and the imagination, and whose universe is peopled with animals who speak and do incredible things?'

I could laugh away the joke storyboards of worms playing head ball at the feeding of the 5000, produced by one group of animators or a proposal to end the nativity episode with a shot of the sky and stars coalescing to make 'Merry Christmas from the Story Keepers'. I was also able to laugh away an alternative ending in the kitchen featuring the 'jolly fat man with the white beard and the red coat giving out presents'. But when we see published biblical animations in the recontextual mode I find I have no answer to the academics' disturbing question. It is difficult enough when the MacGuffin is as unremarkable as children stepping back through time travel, or even the slightly more reality-stretching ride back via a personal computer. But when, as in one script I saw recently, the means of entrée is the adventures of a group of talking, wisecracking animals, the answer becomes impossible to find. It is gratifying that, as a result of *The Story Keepers*, many former academic sceptics have been won over, even if some writers and producers remain to be convinced.

The second of the models of biblical animation available in 1988 I termed the decontextual model. In those early days I stressed the importance of integrity in the presentation of the

What the critics said.

'Compared to some of the brainwashing that goes on in religious productions this stands in a better position than most.'

Times Educational Supplement, 16 October 1998

'These are simply the best religious programmes for children yet made.'

Methodist Recorder, 18 June 1998

'. . . early Christians were story-tellers . . . stories were visibly and obviously an essential part of what they were and did . . .'

N. T. Wright, *The New Testament and the People of God* (1992)

'. . . getting the "feel" right – that the stories weren't told out of idle curiosity, but as part of a living (and persecuted) community.'

N. T. Wright, Canon Librarian Westminster Abbey

'. . . the method of creating stories to provide authentic background is excellent. The oral tradition is probably the way it happened . . .'

Michael Skinner, Wesley House, Cambridge

'I found the constant parallels with the Christian community a brilliant idea. The vivacity of the whole is delightful.'

Henry Wansborough, St Benet's Hall, Oxford

'I find the storytelling and the placing of the story in the cultural milieu of the Christian community very appealing.'

Prof. Christopher Rowlands, Queen's College, Oxford

biblical stories and the need to take biblical scholarship seriously; and, superficially, the biblical animations based on this second model seemed to do that. This model takes Bible stories and presents them as straight as possible as stories to be told in their own right as literary artefacts, rather like the stories of other narrative-based literature – the Arabian Nights, Aesop's Fables, the Greek myths, the Canterbury Tales. The stories are told with little or no attempt to place them in any form of context – just as stories, animated as such.

The first concept to catch my attention and start me on my tortuous search for an alternative to these two conventional models was the French notion to present biblical stories in Japanese shadow-theatre animation. At first it looked an interesting and very attractive way through. The artwork and backgrounds were stunningly pretty and original. The stories were simply told and uncomplicated in structure. However, like other animations based upon the decontextual model, whilst being very pretty and delightful to look at, it was based upon what I am increasingly convinced is a false reading of the potential audience and, above all, of the society in which the audience is to be found, particularly in Western Europe.

Those who favour this mode assume that audiences – and as they use the children's medium of animation they have *young* audiences in mind – both have a wish to watch animations of biblical stories and are equipped to decode them. They assume that there is an interest in the traditional biblical stories just as there is in nursery rhymes, fairy stories and other inherited artefacts of the Christian culture into which Western European children are born. They then further assume that, provided the stories are presented interestingly enough, the young in particular will want to watch animations of these parts of their cultural heritage. The assumption is that there is an audience both eager to hear the stories and familiar enough with the biblical tradition, language and presuppositions to be able to understand them without any prior explanation, just like any other traditional secular story.

This may have been the case even as recently as the 1950s, although my research into the religious life and experience of industrial working-class communities tends to support the view that there may well never have been a time when these assumptions could be made for mass audiences. By the 1980s they most certainly could not be made for the television audiences of Western Europe. As a Christian social observer, much as I may regret the trend, I have to recognise that those assumptions are naïve at best and positively harmful at worst. Producers and writers in the decontextual mode are hiding behind cultural tradition and reserved broadcasting slots which schedulers are increasingly desperate to fill. They work hard to prettify their presentation, concentrating on production 'look', whilst ignoring the sociological reality that their audiences are biblically illiterate and lack the background or experience either to want to watch or to appropriate the stories, no matter how prettily they are presented.

As a teacher, educational researcher and parent, I was painfully aware that children acquire literacy skills by hearing words spoken, hearing stories read to them, by watching opinion leaders and role models read, and by being introduced to sounds and symbols in an environment in which the book is valued and words and language are used. Add to that a series of culture-building experiences and the skill of reading is more easily acquired. I was all too aware that acquiring the *biblical* literacy skills so necessary to appropriate biblical information requires the same kind of foundations. Where children grow up in homes or schools in which the Bible is seldom present let alone read; where few adults read the stories to them; where the Bible is not given a place of respect and value and where the parents or teachers do not introduce the children to the faith community in which the Bible is valued and its distinctive stories and language patterns are used, biblical illiteracy is the norm. Many of us grow up in that home/school environment. We understand at first hand the difficulties involved for children in mass television audiences for whom the Bible represents a foreign language and its stories represent an alien culture. We would hesitate to use any stories which merely reinforced that alienation.

My main problem with the decontextual model, however, was theological. Its proponents seem to me to be guilty of ignoring 100 years of biblical scholarship. It is now axiomatic in biblical study to say that the gospels which we have inherited are faith vehicles. They are not objective stories. Nor are the teaching stories, like the parables, neutral. They were told and retold to build up the faith of believers in living communities of people who were profoundly influenced by the central story which dominates them all – the resurrection of Jesus. The stories cannot therefore be regarded as stories like other non-biblical stories.

The central stories of the Christian tradition, the Gospels, are overladen with the beliefs that the tellers had about the central figure, Jesus of Nazareth. In addition, scholars recognise that we have no information about this man from any sources other than those whose whole view about him and his life, their lives and their place in the world, were permanently coloured by their beliefs about him through his resurrection. Thus, the context in which the stories about Jesus were preserved was the lives and experiences of the communities who sought to follow him and to base their lives upon him.

In the same way, the context in which the stories in the Jewish scriptures – tales of national heroes, great historical events in the people's past – were kept alive over centuries was their being told and retold generation by generation, and re-enacted week by week, year by year, in the great religious festivals in the homes of Jewish communities. These stories, later taken on by Christians as part of their religious heritage, cannot legitimately be lifted out of the context in which they began, which preserved them and which passes them on still today. They are simply not the same order of stories as Aesop's Fables or the Arabian Nights. These stories cannot be separated from the group experiences of the communities who told them, nor from the experiences of the story-tellers who lived them out. To lift them out of this living, interacting context of faith, commitment and belief, and treat them as isolated literary artefacts, pages in a book or chapters in a record to be re-presented, dramatised and brought to life in another audio-visual medium, disembodies and ultimately bleeds the stories dry.

When I expressed my theological uneasiness about the implications of the decontextualising model to the writer of an episode of one such animation, he responded with a strange mixture of incredulity and pride: 'Don't tell me you treat the stories as *sacred*, do you?' And the word 'sacred' was said almost mischievously. I smiled. Millions have given their lives to preserve and pass on these stories. He did not know what he was saying.

In rejecting this model as inadequate, particularly for my aim of reaching the unchurched and those outside the faith communities, I was aware that I had nothing else to put in its place. Conversation with Professor James Dunn, a leading British New Testament scholar, in 1989 convinced me that the clue lay in 'context'. This was confirmed by close reading of an exciting new book which he recommended, *The Shadow of the Galilean* by the German scholar Gerd Theissen.[2] This is a book of biblical scholarship, but it is written as a short novel-cum-investigative enquiry based upon the contrived experiences of an imaginary Jew in the later days of the life of Jesus. Given the responsibility by the Roman authorities for making a full report on the peasant preacher from Nazareth, the lead character meets a range of people who have met or have information about Jesus. Jesus himself nowhere appears. But indirectly, by cleverly building up a picture, reporting a number of events and stories about and by Jesus, and reporting the impact he had on a range of contemporaries, from guerrilla fighters to mystics, the main character presents an exciting and arresting portrait of Jesus – his life, work and impact – set

[2] Gerd Theissen, *The Shadow of The Galilean* (SCM Press, 1987).

against the political, cultural and social context in which he lived.

I shared James Dunn's enthusiasm for the Theissen approach and his view that it could well form the basis of a fine screenplay. The imaginative use of characters, dialogue and action set in a real time and place, as the context in and through which the gospel stories might be told, was an exciting concept. I was unhappy, however, about the pre-resurrection context in which Theissen set the stories. For where did Theissen get his information from in the first place, if not from writers who wrote *after* the resurrection and whose vision is permanently affected by those events?

In that same year of 1989 I sent a memorandum to my advisers emphasising the concept of context. For the retelling of stories about Jesus, however, Theissen's pre-resurrection setting was, I felt, inappropriate.

I was aware that scholars have commonly held that the stories which eventually came to be written in the gospels were, for a period of over 40 years after the death and resurrection of Jesus, kept alive within the community of his followers by constant telling and retelling. Some dispute whether the writer of John had access to this oral tradition, but there seems to be a consensus that, before the stories were finally written down, they were told over and over again in meetings and gatherings – particularly over supper – as the story of the last days was told and re-enacted. I knew too that the catalyst for the writing down of the stories was the impact of the first great state-sponsored persecution in Rome under Nero in AD 64. Until then, in the comparatively free and easy and religiously tolerant Roman Empire, the new Christian community could quietly go its own way, live its distinctive lifestyle and continue at its gatherings to tell the stories of its founder. Many of those who were his close friends, and other witnesses to his life, travelled around the Empire and their living voice was listened to with respect.

Nero's decision to turn on the Christians and to lay blame for the fire of Rome upon the Christian community in Rome came as a major shock to the new Church. Paul and Peter were two leading victims of the persecution. They and other witnesses were silenced. There was real danger that the story would be lost for ever, unless someone took the initiative and wrote it down. The lasting aftershock of the persecution formed the context in which the story attributed to Mark was to be written down a year, or perhaps a little more than a year, later.

This was exactly the context I had focused on in Chapter 5 of my book *The Choice*[3], the small workbook published in 1970 to introduce young people to some of the issues underlying Alan Dale's *New World*. I set the chapter entitled 'The Sign of the Fish', amongst a group of Christians in Rome who huddled together secretly for fear of their lives, meeting in each other's homes during the dark days to retell the stories of Jesus. Their secret sign, the fish, which they scrawled on the doors of their clandestine meeting places, represented an early Christian credal statement and summed up the early Church's beliefs about Jesus. The individual letters of the Greek word for fish, *ichthus*, are the first letters of that credal statement 'Jesus Christ Son of God your Saviour'.

That, I said in 1990 at a series of meetings of theologians, biblical scholars and others I convened at the BBC to think through an alternative model, was the MacGuffin I was looking for. That was the way in. That was the context. After the meetings I instructed no fewer than four different scriptwriters: 'Place the stories in the historical context of a story-telling community in Nero's Rome prior to their being written down. Focus on the sign of the fish and all it meant to the early Christian story-tellers.' These were all highly experienced – in two cases award-winning – writers, but having got the MacGuffin, they did not come up with anything distinctively different from what was already there in the other two models. However, looking back, to be fair to them, neither they nor I realised at the time that it *was* no different. We were unaware of how locked into the old models we

---

[3] See above p. 39. See also Appendix (a).

were. Clearly, I failed to get across to them that I was not looking for a life of Jesus, whereas that was what they were expecting. That was what they were comfortable with. I was clearly talking a foreign language when I talked of the oral tradition. They saw it just as a trick. What they all in their different ways wanted to do was to write a story of Jesus, a picture biography for children. One of them produced Sunday School stories; another a semi-documentary; another a mega-big Cecil B. de Mille-type drama, full of imaginative action and dialogue.

They all, in varying degrees, offered a life of Jesus, wrapped in the decorative paper of a story-teller telling stories about the prophet from Nazareth at a series of clandestine meetings of persecuted followers, hiding from Nero's persecution below the city of Rome. The backstory of the persecution provided the setting for the story-telling and the reason why the listeners were hiding away. It was, however, no more than the hook to catch the viewer's attention before we got on to the real thing – the life of Jesus. The scriptwriters ignored the BBC group's scholarly memorandum: they mixed stories from the various gospel sources with abandon; they created imaginary characters and dialogue in biblical stories; and more worryingly, they portrayed incidents and events unquestionably literally, and ignored all the scholarly suggestions about the texts and traditions upon which I had been insisting. I rejected the offerings in despair. I had thought that we had left all that behind in the 1970s, but clearly I was wrong.

For these writers the backstory served the same function as the imaginary fantasy situation in the recontextual model. It opened the door into the real purpose of the show – a good old decontextualised story from the life of Jesus. It was also interesting to see that the production company which rushed out their three episodes using the title and concept I was developing couldn't escape from the dominant models either.

In addition, because, at that time, we were still thinking of 52 five-minute episodes with one story of Jesus in each, the wraparound was as peripheral as possible and the content of the Bible passage as decontextualised as if it had no introductory setting. The story-teller was disembodied as a voice-over. He or she had no individuality, no personal adventure or story, no involvement in the story because his or her role was essentially introductory and subordinate to the main content – the biblical story itself. The stories inevitably were taken as given, and the order of the story as outlined in the three synoptic gospels, first set by Mark, was followed slavishly.

We produced a five-minute pilot, using a new script by Robin Lyons on the Feeding of the Five Thousand, with the mellifluous voices of David Suchet telling the story and Anthony Hopkins as the voice of Jesus. Then we wondered why it did not work any more than did the models I was trying to replace. We wondered why it failed to catch or hold attention, and produced the glazed-over look of practised, concealed boredom reserved for school religious assembly. We had poured almost $60,000 into the pilot. We had the best voices and probably the most experienced director in Europe. But despite that, I will live with the memory of the sympathetic but cruel-to-be-kind reactions of the professionals whose hopes, after my enthusiastic build-up, were so cruelly dashed by the resulting five-minute pilot video.

Whilst I was licking my wounds my son-in-law Andrew Melrose, who was researching modern English literature at the time, telephoned out of the blue. He knew that I was quite depressed by the failure to break through and by the general feeling that we had got it all wrong. He began to talk about developments in post-modernism and other movements in literary criticism with their emphasis upon 'story', and about their implications for our search for a model for presenting biblical stories in animation.[4] I do not pretend to have understood fully what he was saying. Even after I talked with the Oxford

---

[4] See Brian Brown, 'Right at Last: Keeping the Gospel Stories Alive', *Viewpoints* (March 1977), pp. 5–6

theologian Tom Wright, who devotes large chunks of his recent books to the significance of post-modernist literary research for the study of the life of Jesus, I am not certain I fully grasp it. Put quite simply, however, Andrew said that if we take seriously what literary critics are saying, we have got our emphasis in the wrong place. They would agree with our emphasis on the context: the stories told are fine. But, he said, developments in the literary field would suggest that we should switch our emphasis away from what was told to who was telling it.

What Andrew was saying struck a chord for me with movements in contemporary biblical study. Biblical scholars, too, are now focusing upon story.[5] However, the so-called redaction critics are also drawing our attention to the role played by the authors of the gospels in shaping the stories into the form in which we have them now. They too are drawing our attention to those who told the story.

Since Albert Schweitzer wrote his famous demolition of the search to find the historical Jesus almost 100 years ago, we have all taken as given that we simply do not have the materials – in fact we have no objective historical materials – to write, let alone dramatise, a life of Jesus. Biblical scholars gave up the attempt to write a historical life of Jesus long before Zeffirelli put scholarship back 100 years with his classic *Jesus of Nazareth*. What we have, instead of history or biography, is a series of stories of certain events and other teaching stories, preserved orally for over 40 years, which were later committed to writing for fear that the stories would be lost for ever. Those who finally wrote the stories down put their own spin, or the spin of the communities for which they published, on the materials they had to hand (mainly oral, but there is some evidence to suggest that there were some documents available), and set them within their own

---

[5] N. T. Wright, *The New Testament and the People of God* (SPCK, 1992), pp. 25–26.

framework.[6] That ordering of the materials is what scholars call their redaction.

Thus, although he is a scholar in English, not New Testament, Andrew's suggestion that we focus more on the story-teller intriguingly chimed in with what biblical scholars were saying about how the gospel documents came down to us. If we were going to set the series in the period which stimulated the church to publish the first formal collection of those isolated oral stories – if we were going to contextualise the stories – we should tell the story of the story-teller in the context in which he told his stories. In other words, we had to put flesh upon the disembodied voice of the story-teller, create not just a locus for his story-telling but a whole storyline of situations in which the story-telling took place.

Andrew's suggestion that the fleshed-out story-teller be a Jewish baker in Rome, combined with the brilliant drawing of Len Simon, a young Canadian art director with Don Bluth in Dublin, resulted in the emergence of the icon, Ben the Baker, the heroic leader of the underground church in Rome. The BBC pilot had the embryonic situation of the story-teller-within-a-persecuted-community; it had the suggestion of a family context. It needed an icon and an iconic family – a wife and a group of children temporarily separated from their real parents, fostered in a bakery and hidden in the underground catacombs – to start us on the road towards the new concept we were seeking.

As most of the Christians in Rome, as elsewhere, were Jewish by birth and the gospel stories first began to circulate in Galilee, it was right that our main icon should be Jewish and that his father would have been a baker before him in Galilee. One of the most prominent stories involving loaves of bread in the gospels took place in Galilee, a hotbed of unrest and simmering revolt throughout much of the first half of the first century after the

---

[6] See Gerd Theissen and Annette Merz, *The Historical Jesus: A Comprehensive Guide* (SCM Press, 1996).

birth of Jesus. The event in this story, a large meal in a grassy place in the hills, some scholars suggest, may have been attended by some of the men of violence who lived in the hills planning insurrection, and who may have seen the popular healer and prophet from Nazareth as a possible leader. Whatever the truth of that speculation, all agree that a central character in the story of this meal was not one of the men of violence. It was a little boy who brought rolls or loaves of bread to the meeting. We have no evidence that this boy was the son of a baker who sent him to listen to this great prophet. We have no evidence that later this boy grew up, became a baker himself and was forcibly expatriated to set up a shop in Rome. Nor that he became a follower of the great prophet before he left Galilee. But we have no evidence that he did not. There seemed nothing to prevent our using dramatic licence to develop that imaginative backstory into a more fleshed-out faction story in its own right around a central character, our iconic hero Ben Ami, 'son of the Land'.

The faction situation and the first fleshed-out character having emerged, we moved to establish the rest of our central story characters. Those New Testament scholars who have focused their enquiries into the oral and documentary sources available to the authors of the gospels tell us that we have not only the stories written down by Mark, which were in circulation during the persecution and, by common agreement, were probably written down in the years immediately after that traumatic event, but we also have those stories later to be written down by Luke. These were, notably, the stories of the shepherds and some of the most familiar parables such as the Good Samaritan and the Prodigal Son. These were, Source Historical scholars tell us, probably written down by Luke after Mark's gospel was first published. But these stories were equally likely to have been in oral circulation amongst other Christian communities at the same time as those Mark used.

Internal analysis of the individual gospels suggests that, if Mark was written with a Jewish audience primarily in mind, Luke was probably written with a gentile or a Greek audience in view. It would be likely that Luke's distinctive stories were kept alive orally amongst the smaller numbers of Greek Christians spread widely throughout the Empire, some of whom were intermarrying with fellow Christians who were Jewish by birth.

Left to me as an academic purist, only stories which appear in Mark's gospel would have been used in a series set in Rome in AD 64. I would have left out the great parables of the lost, the Good Samaritan, the Lost Sheep, the Prodigal Son, many of the seven words from the cross. I would even have omitted the nativity stories, the visits of the Magi and the shepherds. However, I was persuaded by broadcasters that there were certain stories without which the public would feel there was not a full life and teaching of Jesus being told. As one BBC producer put it, urging me to include the birth stories: 'They expect a beginning.'

My problem was that so many of my target audience get no further than the beginning. Their experience and knowledge of the story of Jesus begins and ends with nativity plays at school or at the annual carol service. My nightmare was that, if we started with the birth stories, a huge part of the audience would switch off after the first week, their religion having been done! For that same reason, I have also been uneasy about the notion of nativity specials and, left to me and not the marketers, there would have been no *Story Keepers* Christmas video made after I left the production.

I was reminded, too, by various scholars, particularly Professors Kingsley Barrett of Durham and Cecil McCullagh from Belfast, that I should avoid the mixing of sources that characterised many past presentations of the gospels on celluloid or video. Somehow, they pleaded, stories found in Mark had to be seen to be separate and apart from the distinctive stories in Luke and the other gospels. This was particularly important for the nativity stories of the shepherds and the Magi which, unlike in Christmas tableaux, should not be mixed up. So, if we were to be consistent in our attempt to base the script upon the findings of biblical scholarship, and we created an imaginative Jewish baker from Galilee as the main teller of the stories currently in oral circulation in Rome, we needed, I argued, a separate story-teller for those distinctively Lukan stories which were in circulation amongst Greek Christians and which the broadcasters insisted we introduced. As Luke also told stories sympathetic to women it made sense, I argued, for the Lukan story-teller to be a woman. I suggested Ben's wife to be Greek, relatively high born and artistic, and a courier for the stories of Luke. Hence, Helena was created to indicate another tradition and source different from and separate from that represented by her husband.

I do not think that many amongst the production team either understood or cared much about my strange insistence on the separatedness of the various stories. But I got my reward when explaining my idiosyncratic behaviour to a group of theological students in Dublin. One young woman afterwards confessed: 'I always thought all that critical stuff we get in the first term is boring and irrelevant. I saw it for the first time tonight.' A number of teachers using the series with religious studies classes have responded similarly.

The three children we introduced as Ben and Helena's foster 'family' fulfilled no academic function. They represent the vulnerability of the young Christian community and, above all, the fragility of the gospel tradition in the years immediately following the death and resurrection of Jesus. If the 'living voice' of those who could trace back their memories of Jesus to the glory days in Galilee was in danger of being lost for ever, through old age and through violent death, the only hope of preserving the memories, in the absence of a written record, lay in passing on the oral tradition to children. But the young were especially vulnerable during the persecution and needed protection. The adults, then, had a double role to play. They had to pass on the stories. But they had to keep the children safe until the danger to the church had passed. In the experience of the children we see the context of fear mixed with hope, terror mixed with confidence, in which the stories of Jesus were kept alive.

Above all, the fact that Ben, Helena and the adults chose to risk their lives to preserve the stories and to tell them to the children witnesses to the ongoing significance of the story and the one around whom the stories revolve. That the stories were important enough for ordinary folk like Ben and Helena to be willing to die for their preservation, is a strong positive statement in itself. As I write this, I cannot but be struck by the unconscious profundity of the semi-sarcastic incredulity of the writer's question: 'Don't tell me you treat the stories as *sacred*, do you?' I wonder what answer he would have received from those who risked all to keep the stories alive?

The device of telling the stories to the children means that the stories have to be translated into language accessible to mass audiences, and it follows that there is no place for the 'thees and 'thous' of traditional biblical language. Setting the story-telling in a highly charged situation of fear, oppression and violence also immediately places the stories in a real and not a fantasy situation which resonates with the experience, at first or second hand, of many in the audience today. Through the vicarious participation in the traumas experienced by children of their own age in a situation which really happened, and which parallels situations which have occurred and continue to occur throughout history, young viewers are brought face to face with the miracle of the survival not only of the Story but of the people who have kept it alive through the ages.

But how were we to transfer these ideas into drama? Someone had to sit down and write. I had failed to get my ideas across to other writers. We had, in any case, no more money to pay professional writing fees. There was no alternative: one of us had to sit down and draft scripts.

I was not a writer. I had helped reshape *Light of the World* and I had written academic books and some books for young people. But I had not written scripts, certainly not for animation.

Andrew Melrose had not written anything either. I found it relatively easy to select and translate the Bible passages and to present them in language suited to a reading age of 9. But it seemed the height of arrogance to assume that either of us could write a script.

However, there was nothing else to be done. I had watched with admiration Robin Lyons' clever, sparse use of language as he scripted the five-minute piece on the Feeding of the Five Thousand for the BBC pilot. I had seen another writer scripting Bible stories in columns. So in the summer of 1992 I locked myself away, selected the biblical stories required, translated and dramatised them in the way I learned from Robin Lyons, and then dramatised the action into animation. Then, using the character descriptions we had devised, I drafted in longhand 52 episodes of backstory and biblical dialogue, in two columns with dialogue and voice-over on the left and action on the right. The manuscript was then typed up to make Draft 1 of *The Story*, dated June 1992. This was slightly revised during that summer, in the light of comments from my team of advisers, to become the Draft 2 document I was to present to the script-writing team two years later.

For demonstration and sales purposes we also needed a promotional video. Andrew Melrose scripted a voice-over commentary for a three-minute 'promo' (see Appendix (e)), containing 90 seconds of sample animation and character stills to show the style used and to introduce our new iconic family.

Chapter 10

Serendipity

It was at this point, after we had struggled to establish a way through, that serendipity lent a hand again. In 1994 I proudly took Draft 2, a script of 52 five-minute episodes, to our North American writing and production team. The writers were extremely surprised to learn how much we had done and that, in particular, the concept, the characters and the biblical sections were already well developed. Early on we also established that those biblical sections, having been approved and having the names of distinguished scholars attached to them, were sacrosanct. Whatever twists or vagaries the project would follow over subsequent years, those passages remained untouched and inviolable.

Much to my chagrin, however, I learned from our American colleagues that there was no call for five-minute pieces on US children's television or, in particular, on video. I was told that, if we were to meet the deadline, I would have to reshape the whole series into thirteen episodes of 25 or 26 minutes to fit the television half-hour slot.

Our writing team had wide experience of writing for Saturday morning children's television and brought that expertise to the task we were now set. They were to take the evolving concept of biblical story-telling within a real historical context, based upon the adventures of a group of Christians providing shelter for a group of children, two brothers and a girl, in Nero's Rome in AD 64, and adapt it to the three-act format favoured by Saturday morning children's shows. In addition, since the television audience could not be guaranteed to watch week after week and had to be able to drop in and pick up without requiring prior knowledge of previous episodes, each show had to be conceived as complete and one-off. The only constant in the series was the characters; it could not be a serial in which action carried on from week to week. Furthermore as a main market was for the videos, each episode had to be self-standing to allow buyers to pick and mix at will.

I was initially taken aback by the magnitude of the task we had set ourselves as I sat down with the newly appointed Head Writer and executives from the two US co-distributing companies in California. These new requirements meant a complete shift in the mindset I had had for the preceding six years. In a two-day brain thrash, with virtually no more than a blank piece of paper in front of us, the four of us started the creative process to outline the first three episodes, adapting the concept and fleshing out the characters as we went. In my modular career I have often had to adapt and to learn on the job, but this time I had to learn not only new language but also new assumptions, all in the space of two days before I flew 5000 miles back home. And I was the cheerful English amateur trying to hold his head up with experienced and skilled American professionals.

Classic children's animations have traditionally been based on the clash between good and evil, 'goodies' and 'baddies'. The excitement of the adventure revolves around the threat, the near thing, the danger, the capture, the escape; and a resolution of the conflict comes not necessarily by the defeat and destruction of the evil power or person, but by their being subdued, enabling the good character to fight another day. Built up over three acts, this is the action of the typical Saturday morning kids' drama, which is based on two similar models, termed in the writing fraternity as the 'Getting out of Dodge' model and the 'Voyage to the Centre of the Earth' model. In the 'Getting out of Dodge' model the heroes are threatened, all seems to be up, then they get away to fight again next time. That with the 'Voyage to the Centre of the Earth' model, the continual pressing on through threats, near defeats and narrow escapes, seemed to fit what we were looking for.

The Saturday morning kids' drama is essentially an entertaining model, and to use it as a vehicle to tell stories which are culturally significant and, to the faith communities, sacred, entailed a risk which still raises eyebrows in certain quarters. However, I have observed children watching episodes of *The Story Keepers* in a variety of situations from school to church to youth festival to home. I have watched faces and body language. I have noted the finger-biting anxiety in moments of tension; the worried eyes at times of threat; the peals of laughter when the 'goodies' triumph and the tension is relieved. Above all, I have seen the same faces distorted in mirth one minute, absorbed in fascination the next, as in quick succession the drama moves from hilarity to serious presentation of a sacred moment.

The script writers were in a long tradition when they proposed using humour – sometimes deliberately as corny and weak as the average nine-year-old's worst – and often outrageous high slapstick interludes to break the tension in certain scenes which, unrelieved, would have been unbearable for young viewers. At first I, the renegade academic and ex-teacher, was uneasy about the style being developed. But I was the amateur and I bowed to experience. Also, the more I thought about what was happening, the more I saw that we were on to something. The humorous presentation of the coldly evil and increasingly megalomaniac Nero as a figure not of fear but of fun, did not diminish his evil but cut the monster down to size and made him manageable by young minds. The stark reality of the historical context of persecution and abuse of power in the backstories, and the harshness of the events of the life and death of Jesus of Nazareth in the gospel sections, would not, unrelieved, be sustainable by most children. Put within the entertaining Saturday morning kids' format in *The Story Keepers*, however, not only is the reality bearable but, against the backcloth of humour and exciting adventure, the pain and horror are apprehended without in any way having to be concealed.

The model is fast moving action, with scenes changing rapidly and little time to dwell. The supervising director enunciated the principle, 'They must never go to the fridge', meaning that there must never be a time when the young viewer, bored with the lack of compelling action, stands up and goes to get a Coke or a biscuit. In the age of the remote control and a multiplicity of channel options there is no guarantee that 29 per cent audience share can be retained even minute by minute, let alone week by week. Thus, we needed exciting adventures, rapidly – almost breathlessly – told, together with accurately translated, sparsely scripted biblical stories to attract and hold attention, and to make the shows educative, informative and entertaining at the same time.

Over the two days, as a group, we outlined the first three episodes which were passed to the scriptwriters to work up into first drafts of dialogue and action. These drafts, after comments were received, were then written into second drafts of full dialogue which, when approved, were returned for final polish prior to sign-off. The process which evolved seems, with hindsight, so ordered and controlled. At the time, serendipity and chaos theory seemed to be the rule.

Perhaps the most straightforward of our tasks was the development of the characters we took on from Draft 2 and the creation of new characters. The creation of the personification of wickedness and brutality, Nihilus, the senior Roman officer; the weasily, creepy Snivillus alongside the historical Nero; the Oliver Hardy figure of Stouticus; and the earnest converted centurion Tacticus, were brilliant additions by the writing team. The introduction of the black African, Cyrus, was only coincidentally politically correct. It reflected the fact that the church began as a movement of the dispossessed, and the first mission church began in North Africa.

A greater problem for myself was the task I had to perform in less than 15 hours, once the decision had been taken to reshape the material into half-hour episodes. I had to take the 52 five-minute biblical stories I had brought to America and re-order them without changing them – because they had already been approved – spreading them over 13 episodes and making them capable of being integrated into the ongoing backstory, similar to the outline models we had developed for the first three episodes.

Anyone reading the Culham 'Teacher's Guide to *The Story Keepers*' which relates the series to stages in the National Curriculum,[1] will probably assume that the selection of biblical material and the transitions from the backstory to the biblical stories were carefully planned according to a long-designed scheme. In the same way, if they were to observe the change of art style, colour tone and even music which accompanies change from the backstory to the biblical narrative and to the parables, they would assume that that, too, was the result of long, careful pre-planning. On the contrary, I sat down to the task at 6 p.m. on the night before I was to leave for home, and I had to have it ready by the next morning or the writers would be held up.

Two observations were uppermost in my mind as I began. The first was a scholarship issue; the second, creative. The original 52 stories in the screenplays I took to America largely followed the order in Mark's gospel, plus the nativity stories and some of Luke's parables. The so-called Form Historians told us as far back as the 1930s that the gospel stories circulated initially as a body of isolated incidents and teachings which were told and retold in no particular order. The framework, the order, it is suggested, was imposed by the writers, notably Mark. This would mean that, in the 'oral' period, stories would have been told 'on the hoof' as

---

[1] Diana Lazenby, *Story Keepers – A Guide for Teachers* (Culham Educational Institute and Cassell, 1998).

the situation demanded. They were particularly told to reinforce the beliefs that the early Christians had about Jesus, and they could be grouped together as Mark later did under headings:

> Jesus the Wonder-Worker
> Jesus the Healer
> Jesus the Teacher
> Jesus the Saviour.

All these beliefs they summed up in the stories about his birth.

Following that pattern, I sat down in my bedroom and grouped together the biblical sections of episodes 1–5 and 7–9 in sets of three stories to be told 'on the hoof' as the context or the backstory demanded. They were listed in no particular order other than that they were grouped as teaching or wonder-working or healing stories.[2] In all, these sections comprised approximately 22 per cent of the show, or 5–6 minutes of Bible story per episode.

Scholars also suggest that the stories leading up to the events of the last week – the trial, crucifixion and resurrection – constituted a body of continuous narrative, kept alive as such through telling during the holy meals of the Christians. So I reflected that notion by grouping the stories from the transfiguration to the post-resurrection narratives in episodes 10–13. Furthermore, scholars suggest that the nativity stories, which embodied in story form the church's deepest reflection on the person of Jesus, were added later by Luke and Matthew. I reflected this by putting them as a separate episode, not at the beginning but in the middle of the series, running up to the final four episodes on the passion. At least that way, I consoled myself, the audience will have watched five episodes and captured a picture of Jesus the Healer, Wonder-Worker and Teacher before they meet him as the dew-eyed baby. The order of the stories, therefore, while

---

[2] The arrangement appears in pp. 10–12 of *The Series Bible* written by David Weiss and his 'writing room' in 1994. See Appendix (g).

ending, as does Mark's, with the passion narratives, is mine. As one magazine put it, it constitutes 'The Gospel According to Brian'.[3]

In the same way, the shifts of artistic and musical style to reflect the three levels of story used in the series did not come from a period of deep thought. It came from reflection on an ongoing process. I had originally suggested it without much real thought to the advisory group at the BBC. It was not until I had to rearrange the material that the rationale emerged.

Thinking through the arrangement of the materials on the long flight back from Los Angeles, I indulged myself in some lateral thinking and realised that what was emerging were three levels of story and storyline throughout. The first was the faction storyline of Ben and the children, an imaginative story with imaginary characters in a real historical situationThe second was the stories Ben told about Jesus, the stories of Jesus which were preserved as factual record of historical events. The third was the stories Jesus told, the fictional stories with meaning – the parables.

Len Simon, the animation director, had already created two styles of animation to express the Ben stories and the Jesus stories in the pilot. Simply because the artistic director at that time was more comfortable with it, the pilot had used classic Disney animation for the faction characters and, because I felt uncomfortable with big eyes and exaggerated features, we stuck to the more realistic style for the biblical characters. I had always argued that the stories of Jesus were different, in tone as well as in content, from other stories. I had insisted that we develop a realistic-looking Semitic character, one who was recognisably Jewish and, in skin tone, dress and hairstyle as close as possible to what scholars

---

[3] This phrase was first used in the *Telegraph Magazine*, 6 April 1996, in an article of the same title by Maureen Cleave. It was used again in an article in the *Times Educational Supplement Friday Magazine*, 16 October 1998 pp. 12–13.

suggest he would have looked like. Showing a set of the designs to a group of publishers at a Christian convention in the United States I proudly pointed to the eyes and nose of our markedly Semitic figure, dressed not in a dressing gown but in the short tunic favoured by Galilean men in New Testament times. I felt a face leaning over and heard a voice walking away: 'But Wilmer! He looks Jewish!' Looking at the blue-eyed Nordic representations of the Messiah elsewhere in the hall I sympathised with the poor man's anguish. But I am sure we were right to go for the Jewish look in our designs and the realistic stylings which went with them. The animators may have found them difficult to draw and to animate smoothly. But, at least, conceptually they were less offensive than many other distinctly cartoony designs I had seen.

With these two styles of animation already in use, it was an easy step to add a third style for the parables. However, although the idea of having three different animation styles came to me by a process of lateral thinking on the long flight back from California, it was only afterwards that I developed the theory behind the idea. By the time I arrived in the studio the following week I was articulating the rationale behind the styles for the faction stories and the Jesus stories. It was some time later, when working on the parable of the Sower with an American expatriate artist, Hal Clay, that I remembered what Alan Dale used to say about the humour of Jesus: Jesus' parables were often clever jokes. 'Whoever thought of camels going through eyes of needles?', he used to ask.

I used to hold informal seminars with the new creative team in the reorganised studio when I would try to explain what a story was all about. These seminars were far more stimulating and thought-provoking than any discussions I had had with my degree students, and it was here I hit on the idea of developing an artistic, 'jokey' style of design for the parables, and it seemed to work. It was appealing to look at and captured the light humour Jesus used to get his points across. The animators and creative people thought the style was attractive for the 'look', although

I am less sure that, while indulging my whim, they always understood my reasoning. However, many teachers have said that they
value this stylistic change as an important aid to understanding.
They find it helpful to point to the different artistic styles to ex-
amine in classroom and group work the different types of material which make up the gospel tradition.

Although the series is proving a useful tool in teaching, I would
have to admit the part played by serendipity in the apparently
carefully pre-planned pedagogy which has emerged. The evolution of the title *The Story Keepers* itself is my favourite example of
the theory following haphazard practice. Originally I had wanted
to use the title *The Story*, the title used on Draft 2. As a working
model it was fine. It was capable of a range of meanings. It was the
story of Jesus. It was God's story. It was the story of God's revelation in human form. It was the story which came down to us. Jesus
was *the* story. But not long before we were to go public, well after
we had started the writing and storyboarding and were on the way
with the first animation, we heard that the copyright authorities in
Washington had rejected the title because there were already a
number of books and films in existence using *The Story* in the title:
The Neverending Story, *The Greatest Story Ever Told*, etc.

We tried everything, but no one came up with a new, snappy
title. By the time we were ready to go public with the first three
episodes we still had no overall title. The four Americans and I on
the Point Team found ourselves at 9 a.m. one Friday morning
sitting in a conference room at Fox studios in Los Angeles. We
had a blank whiteboard in front of us and a deadline of 5 p.m. to
come up with a title for release by the publicity people on the
following Monday. I was booked on the flight back next day,
Saturday.

For a full morning we simply threw words against the
whiteboard in the hope that something would emerge. Three
o'clock arrived. We still had no title. Then one of us – I like to
think it was me, but doubtless someone else will claim it was
them! – spotted two words in the left and right corners, 'Story' and

'Keepers'. At first, combining these two words did not make any sense. It was a made-up nonsense expression. But as the next hour went on we kept saying it. It tripped off the tongue all right. We had nothing more attractive. The deadline was now less than an hour away. In desperation we agreed to go with it. The waiting PR men had their title. It was the best we could come up with.

On the flight back I began again the long internalising process of lateral thinking. I slowly came to see the theological and historical sense behind the newly created term and the newly created people. They were those who kept alive 'The Story'. They were those who, through their lives and throughout the ages, have continued to keep The Story alive. They were those who kept The Story of Jesus alive by telling and retelling it. The church is a Story-keeping community.

Since then the title has had an appeal we never dreamed of because of its appropriateness and its contemporary significance. The Scripture Union published a resource pack for church holiday and mid-week clubs containing a video of five *Story Keepers* episodes and a series of group activities set in the catacombs and market place of Nero's Rome.[4] The pack was extremely successful and brought the stories of the gospels close to the experience of vast numbers of British children who might otherwise not have heard them. I visited one such holiday club and was startled to hear the leader address the children as 'fellow Story Keepers'. I smiled as I remembered that hard day in Los Angeles which produced the name they now proudly wore on their badges and T-shirts.

It did not occur to any of us that day, as we shot to the bottom of the lift, that we were adding a new expression for Christian disciples to the English language.

---

[4] John Stephenson, *The Story Keepers Activity Resource* (Scripture Union, 1997).

Chapter 11

Culture clashes

The Point Team met regularly throughout production. The team consisted of the Head Writer, David Weiss, an experienced feature writer who had previously worked for Don Bluth, and three others of us representing the three financing companies – the Irish company set up through the Irish film tax shelter to produce the series, and two US video distributors. We were joined on occasion by the Supervising Director, Jimmy T. Murakami, by Andrew Melrose and a representative of the American publisher. Although not technically co-producers – the production being fully financed in Dublin – the US video distributors through the Point Team exercised a major influence on the look, tone and content of the final product.

At these meetings, which began with the major decision to redesign to fit the needs of the North American video and Saturday morning television audiences, the differing philosophical, theological and cultural assumptions of the three partner groups, North American, Irish and British, were evident from the outset. That the end product appears so unified is tribute to the good sense and mature intelligence of the participants: on the face of it, the whole enterprise appeared to be the disaster waiting to happen which led other similar ventures to founder.

As religion is a dominant force in any culture, a religious television product will reflect the religious situation of the

culture and the audience to which it is directed. The three
groups came from, and produced for, totally different cultures. It was understandable that they had different audiences
in mind for the series we were creating, and therefore differing expectations as to the requirements of 'their market'. It is
clear that left to themselves and not forced by financial needs
to co-operate in the production, each group represented
would have produced a different concept, format and approach to presenting of the biblical material. It was fortunate
that, by the time the meetings of the Point Team began, a lot
of research, Bible translation and selection, concept and character design had been set in stone. I, at least, had a fair idea of
where I was heading, even if, because of my academic's neu-
rotic unwillingness to be satisfied, I appeared to oscillate and
shift continually. My main role in the resulting production
was probably in protecting what I saw as the integrity of the
content in the face of constant pressure from the writers and
artists and, above all, from the marketers, to diverge from it.

The teaching of the Bible is banned in American non-Christian
schools. The churches and Christian families take responsibility
for teaching Bible stories to children. For the relatively high
percentage of North Americans who attend church, their
Christian faith plays a very significant role in their lives. This has
led to the growth of a highly commercial Christian publishing
and, in particular, Christian video market, whose needs and
customer profile were uppermost in the minds of those on the
Point Team representing the North American video distributors.
Those purchasing – or, more often, those whose parents
purchased for them – from the Christian bookstores associated
with the Christian Booksellers Association would have a positive
attitude to the content of the stories, would be equipped to
decode them and appropriate them, and would certainly not be
coming to the stories fresh. They may have had the stories as
staple diet in their acculturation and could well be growing tired
of them. Their parents would be constantly looking for new

ways of telling the stories, and would be looking for some form of recontextualised style of video to put before their children.

One would, however, have to make vastly different assumptions about the British religious situation. Britain has a long history of statutory religious education and religious examinations, and an established, reserved slot for religious broadcasting in an otherwise increasingly secular society, with poorly attended churches served by a relatively small Christian publishing and video market. Viewing this situation of biblical illiteracy and the need to provide material through television to counter children's ignorance of the romance of the gospels' creation and preservation, and to introduce the stories to them, my objective was very different from that of my American colleagues, and my list of priorities was consequently quite different too.

We both also had different audiences in mind from those in Catholic Ireland where the church has a high profile in both family and school life, where religious broadcasting is still significant, and where the Bible, if not read regularly, would still take a revered place in most homes. Priests, theologians and broadcasters in Ireland to whom I spoke were, however, unconvinced that biblical illiteracy was any less a problem in the Republic than it seemed to be in rest of the European Union.

This tension of target audiences and expectations remained throughout the production period, but because the concept was intriguing to all, the tension was creative. For, just as the differences were recognised early on, so the possibilities of the concept to meet the differing needs also quickly emerged. The result was that, rather than being a stumbling-block, this continual tension served to strengthen the concept as it was refined to meet the various needs of the participants and their markets.

The protection given both to religious video publishers in the United States by the voracious and highly profitable Christian publishing market, and to European religious television programme makers by the need to fill religious slots on public broadcasting, has frequently given a false sense of security to

Christian writers and producers, and shielded them from the commercial pressures faced by producers of non-religious material. When George Carey, the Anglican Archbishop of Canterbury, exclaimed, after seeing the first video of *The Story Keepers*, 'Brian, it's so professional!', I knew what he meant. I took it as a compliment and a tribute to the work of the Point Team.

What enabled the Point Team to come together and produce a 'professional' product despite such seemingly irreconcilable cultural tensions, was that we all took the risk which the concept demanded of us. From the very beginning we cast aside the protections of our differing market situations. I knew that in the multi-channel age, where children have a multiplicity of choices on a Sunday morning from terrestrial, cable and satellite programming, there is now no such thing as the reserved slot. When ITV decided to schedule *The Story Keepers* for 10.15 on a Sunday morning, we were head to head with Warner, Fox Kids, the Children's Channel, the BBC, Channel 4 and Channel 5, to name but a few of the options available on British television. Our American colleagues knew that for them too the old securities had gone: the harsh wind of commerciality would blow hard when the video was released.

For us all, the emerging contextual model offered the opportunity to present the gospel stories to our distinctive markets in new and challenging ways. We were no longer relying on the comfort of the safe material with which our protected markets had until now been fed. We were taking a huge risk. We were also breaking the mould. We were offering a totally new way of presenting biblical material, taking scholarship seriously, but also taking the production values of high quality children's Sunday morning entertainment equally seriously.

To those who were long familiar with the stories we were saying: 'Here are the familiar stories told accurately and carefully, but within the historical and cultural context in which they were preserved, as you have never heard or seen them before.' To those who would not normally read, listen to, or watch biblical stories we were saying: 'Here are stories kept alive under the pressure of persecution and which have been passed down to us by people who had real-life adventures in so doing.' Our markets and target audience had one thing in common. Neither previously had been exposed to this new model. It was a risk worth taking and one which has proved the faith that the Point Team placed in it.

This does not mean that the differing cultural stances did not rear their heads throughout the deliberations of the Point Team. They did frequently. But most of the time these issues were containable by compromise and by mutual respect. They were, frankly, not of sufficient gravity to merit a run of the Reformation. When the Irish and Spanish artists, who were used to establish some of the early biblical scenes, reflected the long tradition of Roman Catholic iconography in their cultures in designing Jesus with a far-away, other-worldly look in his eyes, or when they portrayed John the Baptist as reverently pouring water from a dish over the head of Jesus at his baptism rather than plunging him into the waters of the River Jordan, alternative presentations were suggested, discussed and accepted with little difficulty. Equally, it seemed to some of us that the American writers, reflecting current political and social concern for so-called 'family values' in contemporary American society, seemed, in their choice of language, tones of voice and assumptions, to be presenting our iconic 'family' as mirrors of the values and lifestyle of 'Middle America'. This, we feared might lay us open to accusations of cultural imperialism, similar to those aimed by sociologists of knowledge at the creators of Donald Duck and the Disney Empire. But in these cases, suggestions for a little reshaping here and toning down there were received relatively uncontentiously.

The cry of 'cultural imperialism' was heard, however, as soon as the video of the first three episodes was tested on an audience of teachers in English schools! Our American colleagues, with more than a tinge of regret, dug their heels in over the accents used in the voice-over track. They said forcibly and persuasively that American children would not under any circumstances accept English voices – even the Oscar-winning name talent I had lined up. I gave in to the force of the argument but met strong objections from English parents and teachers, at first. As is my practice, I then took the show on the road and set up a series of test situations in schools. As their troubled teachers looked on, the children received the American voices without a murmur. When I questioned them further their response was delightfully summarised by one wise-beyond-his-years nine-year-old: 'It's like opera. You expect that to be in Italian. We expect cartoons to be in American.' There was no answer to that.

It was, however, my insistence, following many hours of meetings with theologians and leaders of a range of churches, upon a non-interpretative approach to the biblical stories which both retained the support of the mainstream of the churches and created most difficulties for me in my role as protector of the integrity of the rationale of the series. This more than anything else threatened the carefully built consensus. I had set out to avoid any one theological interpretation of the stories, and I sought always to present the stories in such a neutral manner that interpretation could be left to the user or viewer. I am aware that sociologists would say that even my neutral stance is equally loaded and that my aim was fraught with problems. I nonetheless felt it would prevent unnecessary dispute. Scholars seem agreed that, by the time the stories came to be written down, they had been told over and over again so many times that the shape, if not the order of the stories, had become set. I felt able to keep close to text in my translations because the stories which we have in Mark's and the other two synoptic gospels would have been the stories current in Rome in AD 64 which, in turn, was our chosen historical context. The text as we have it would by that time have been fairly well established.

I also decided not to add new characters or events in the biblical sections to those which we had in the gospels. This has always been the temptation for dramatists and particularly film makers. The odd additional disciple here; the extra Roman officer there; the imaginative dialogue between disciples or even with Jesus; the dramatic licence with the courtiers of Herod. These have been the classic creations not only of Hollywood movie makers but also of European film producers. This was the approach used in many biblical films up to the 1970s. Now 30 years of scholarship on, this neo-biographical rewriting of the gospels is dismissed as old-fashioned and unhelpful.

These decisions not to amend or interpret the text were welcomed by church advisers. So, too, was the minimalist approach to the telling of the parables. As a teacher I saw the significance of the emphasis that the Form Historians placed upon distinguishing between what they saw as the story that Jesus told and the interpretation added to it. I am less concerned as to whether Jesus added the interpretations himself or whether they were added by the church as what the scholars called 'church words'. As a teacher I would refrain from pointing out *any* morals to children. Children listen to stories and draw their own lessons, which frequently are different from those that we adults draw. I can see why people in the church, or even the writers themselves, may have wanted to add an interpretation to the parable of the Sower or of the Last Judgement. I am personally less convinced (though I recognise I could well be wrong) that so skilled a story-teller and teacher like Jesus would have added interpretations, particularly the kind that appear attached to the parables. On one classic occasion He was asked a question: 'Who is my neighbour?' He gave no answer. He told a story. Afterwards, instead of giving the answer he threw back the question to the man who had posed it. When the man gave his answer, Jesus did not say, 'That is correct.' He left the man to decide for himself on the basis of the story, and said, 'Now you go and do the same.' That is what children are inclined to do when they hear a story.

I am not sure that my reasoning was fully understood. But the minimalist approach of omitting the 'church words' and leaving the stories to speak for themselves had the virtue of holding the conservative and the liberal factions in the churches in some form of unity. So I resisted all attempts from writers or producers to add anything, even by way of asides and comments from the faction story-tellers when telling the stories to the children. I certainly resisted the temptation to add anything to the stories of Jesus.

The only real dispute we had within the Point Team arose over the story of the Lost Sheep, one of the three Parables of the Lost in Luke's gospel so loved by evangelical preachers.[1] In Luke's gospel the story is concluded with the text: 'In the same way there is more happiness in heaven because of one sinner who repents than over ninety-nine good people who don't need to.' I did not think that that comment would be understood by the children. Nor did I think they would come to that conclusion themselves from a simple story about a farmer happy that he found his straying sheep. They would not understand what angels in heaven were, let alone 'sinners'. I dug my heels in and stuck with my minimalist translation ending with the farmer celebrating with his neighbours. I am happy for teachers, parents and preachers to add the missing verse in their discussion with children. I prefer to leave such theological interpretation to others. Far better to tell the story barely, leaving the great questions to speak for themselves.

I had less trouble from the writers and the production team, however, than from the marketing people. The tension between the integrity of the product and its marketability grew more acute as the production proceeded. It first reared its head in an apparently innocent enquiry from a publisher, who was seeking permission to use the characters being developed in the series in a family edition of a Bible. The proposal was to dot the characters throughout the Old and New Testament sections of a published modern translation, to introduce the idea of the family telling or

---

[1] Luke 15:7.

reading Bible stories together. The popularity and customer-friendliness of the characters were seen as ploys to give credibility, in the eyes of families and children, to the biblical stories.

To me it seemed odd to use the characters to endorse stories told in language different from that used in the television series: the one was a modern translation by a group of scholars for use in public worship and private devotion, the other, mine, a translation from the Greek into animation. It also seemed odd to use them to endorse a rival product. Most of all, however, the proposal ignored the basis of the series' concept and its rationale, and I had to ask the marketers some pointed questions. If what underlies the rationale of *The Story Keepers* is that, until Nero's persecution, Matthew, Luke and John, and even Mark, had not been committed to writing, what would Christians in AD 64 be doing endorsing gospels which had not been written at that point in history? What, above all, are they doing endorsing epistles by John and writings like Revelation which few scholars accept as being in existence in AD 64? If we are saying that the Story Keepers kept alive the stories of Jesus what would they be doing telling stories of Genesis, Exodus and the Old Testament corpus when, in the whole of the series, they make no mention of the Old Testament?

Looking back now, the battles with the marketers were only to be expected. Len Simon and his designers had given the marketers a gift from heaven – merchandisable characters: a jolly, rotund, beaming baker, a winsome appealing infant, and other figures which, if it were a secular product underpinned by no distinctive religious scholarship, concept or rationale, could appear on anything from puzzles to pyjamas. And worldwide television windows available to boot! It was Christmas come early. After so much intellectual struggle, however, my reaction was just as predictable. I fired off a fierce defence of the rationale and urged that any developments, whether merchandising or new programming, should be concept-driven and not market-driven.

That remained my dictum throughout the period in which I was associated with the production.

Undeterred, the marketing people came back again. They reported that there was a demand in the marketplace for Old Testament stories to get the *Story Keepers* treatment. It was gratifying to have the commerciality of the series recognised and it was immensely flattering to be asked to create a follow-up series. I was in the middle of a period of hospitalisation when the discussions began and I came late into them. When I did, however, I maintained my original position. *The Story Keepers* was the result of a continually evolving rationale and concept. The characters in the series were given their credibility by their work and role as keepers-alive of the stories of Jesus, and throughout the 13 episodes they did not once mention the Old Testament. For them suddenly to start telling Old Testament stories was, in my view, intellectually inconsistent at best, dishonest at worst.

Besides, the stories they told in *The Story Keepers* were kept alive orally. They were in danger of being lost for ever precisely because they were not written down. Their adventures were caused by their being persecuted because they were keepers-alive of the Story of Jesus. The Old Testament stories, on the other hand, were already written down and had been read from scrolls for generations. They were not the cause for which Christians were prepared to lay down their lives.

The Old Testament stories are Jewish stories. It is true that our central hero, Ben, was born Jewish, but he is a converted Jew who tells Christian and not Jewish stories. Without a massive switch, were we to use the same characters as the marketers wanted, to tell stories sacred to the Jewish faith from which Ben had converted and which Helena, a Greek, had never espoused? I feared we were in danger of being grossly insulting to the Jewish population. But, primarily, we were being cavalier in our use of the concept we had developed over the past eight years. I was affronted that such a notion was even being considered – and for commercial, not academic, reasons.

Any follow up to *The Story Keepers* would, in any case, face two insurmountable problems. Firstly, if we follow the rationale closely, we have to recognise that the faction stories of Ben and the children were located in a particular time and historical situation. That is what makes them what they are. They make no sense outside that context. In the same way, although it would be relatively easy to devise new adventures, if we are to take what scholars say about the way the gospels were handed on to us seriously, we must limit the biblical stories told to those current in Rome in AD 64. That is, we should use only what came to be Mark's gospel and perhaps some parables from Luke. We have used most of those stories already in the first *Story Keepers*.

Secondly, the option offered by the marketers – to place the characters in a later time – faces the problem that children age. Four-year-old Marcus would be less cute as an eight-year-old in AD 68. Pre-teen Anna would be a young woman and beyond the age when viewers under the age of nine could identify with her. We cannot use the same children, if we set the stories later, without intellectual dishonesty. Besides, *The Story Keepers* concludes at episode 13. The stories are finished. Anna has left. Cyrus, Marcus and Justin are reunited with their parents. Tacticus and his wife have moved on. The evil Nihilus is dead. Ben and Helena are in exile. It is stretching credibility to have *Son of Story Keepers* or some other follow-up when the original series came to a definite conclusion.

In response, the marketers suggested that, like *Star Wars*, we should develop a new concept – a prequel, setting the adventures amongst a new group of those who produced Ben and the Story-keeping community in the past. They could not, however, answer my questions: in what location, at what time, in what situation do you place the telling of a story no one knew was going to happen until it did, which only God in his providence controlled? How can you focus on a community in Israel when no one could predict that Jesus would come or, most of all, that one of this community's descendents would become a follower of Jesus, become a baker, be shipped to Rome and, under Nero, would set up an underground church?

As a last desperate resort the marketers began to talk of a movie involving the same characters but – and here their suggestions not only lacked understanding of the concept and rationale but bordered on impiety – having adventures without any reference to biblical stories. I tried to imagine the concept of keepers-alive of the Story who do not tell any stories, and who have adventures keeping alive a story they do not mention. I found it somewhat difficult.

I may have convinced myself of the academic purity of my argument but I do not for a moment believe I have won the commercial argument with the marketers. It is quite possible that, now I have left the project, the sheer commerciality of a prequel or *Son of Story Keepers* will be pushed by others less sensitive to the theological, historical or biblical rationale, whose motivation is commercial and not evangelical. I will sit in my corner and despair. But I will not regret the stand I took.

Chapter 12

Time to move on

On 19 September 1997, eight months after ITV first screened *The Story Keepers*, at a meeting convened by Churches Together in England, Paul Corley, ITV's controller responsible for religious programming, publicly asked me to reconsider my view on a follow-up to *The Story Keepers*. I had publicly stated that I did not wish to do any further series. I had achieved my aim. I had realised my vision. I rehearsed all the reasons why I considered the concept of a follow-up to *The Story Keepers* was intellectually untenable. Paul, who had been largely instrumental in ITV taking the then commercially risky decision to acquire the series, none the less wished to persuade me to think again.

I had to take his plea seriously. We had known each other since my days working on Channel 4's pop show *The Tube*, which he produced. It was divine serendipity that, the day I arrived to present the series to ITV, he had just taken over as Deputy Controller. To be met not only by a familiar, friendly face but by a broadcaster I knew had vision, integrity and courage, made me believe the series was going to happen after all. Throughout and since production he has been a firm friend who believed in what I was doing and supported my efforts to maintain integrity throughout. For months after the meeting I wrestled with his public challenge.

It took me a further two years of research, rethinking and consultation to come up with a format and a concept to tell Old Testament stories in the contextual mode. That involved being honest and ditching the commercially attractive *Story Keepers* characters and the setting in Nero's Rome for a new setting and new lead characters – and even a new title. It meant following the intellectually and morally more honourable route than that offered by the marketers. It meant asking all the troubling questions about concept, format, setting and rationale again, and coming up with new answers.

The key issues which underlie the rationale in the new cycle I have created arose whilst the original series was being made. They have been mulled over and analysed and now are part of the further rationale which is emerging. The first arose as early as the first Point Team meetings when we were outlining the action of episode 3, 'Catacomb Capers', in which we introduce the story of the Good Samaritan. The natural progression was to develop action and a backstory, exploring the themes of the dilemma and response of the Samaritan faced with the wounded enemy in the mountain road. The transition from the backstory to the biblical story which increasingly became a concern to me as the first episodes were outlined and scripted, was made smoother because the theme of the backstory action sprang directly out of the theme of the biblical story. In the email conversations I had with the Head Writer after he sent his team's suggested outlines for episodes 4, 5 and 7, I argued that the Bible stories should not just be dropped in, almost as an afterthought, but that the theme of the biblical stories should determine the overall theme.

Although I did not pick up the significance of what we were doing at the time, as episodes 8 and 9 came to be outlined, I suggested that we follow the same procedure as we followed in episode 3 and draw out the backstory from the theme of the biblical story. The winsome tale of the circus boy Cyrus, attracted by the fame of being a top performer for the wicked slave owner, then things going wrong when the slaves revolt and he finds himself outside, homeless in the street, was closely modelled on the theme of the Prodigal Son. Similarly, the theme of the parable of the Tenants in the Vineyard provided the theme for the adventure based on Nero's birthday party in episode 9. In the same way, and perhaps more significantly, the themes of the events of the last week of Jesus' life, his betrayal, his trials, his death and resurrection, were directly reflected in the storylines for the adventures of Ben and his family in episodes 10–13. I was glad that critics recognised not only the better quality of animation in those later episodes but the greater tightness in the structure of the storylines and the writing. This modification of the rationale to allow for closer interaction of the theme of the biblical story and the backstory has been taken over into the outlines of the new series which are far more dependent on the theme of the biblical stories than were some of the early episodes of *The Story Keepers*.

As the *Story Keepers* episodes developed, so did the characters. Had the series moved on and retained the same characters, there is no doubt that character development would have had a high priority. By the end of the series some of the characters were already in process of modification because of the action in earlier episodes. They were developing their personalities and traits under their own steam. A prime example is the boy Justin who, relatively anonymous in early episodes, develops as a story-teller and gains in personality as a result. The greater concentration upon themes, storylines and character in the new series has resulted in a major shift in the concept and rationale for the series. This time I have written the themes, the storylines and detailed character studies in advance of the scripting commencing.

It is no coincidence that I am working for the new series with the leading American writer of soap operas. By bringing the distinct soap-opera emphases upon character, character development and storyline over a block of episodes, she is bringing a new dimension to the scripts, transforming the concept once more. Cultural analysts point to the way in which the soap opera, perhaps the most distinctive contribution made by radio and television to drama, appears to speak most vividly to viewers because of the closeness of the storylines and overarching themes to everyday experiences of audiences. Stories become part of conversation and gossip because they are seen to resonate with the real life-and-death experiences of mass audiences. In the same way, many Biblical scholars talk of the eternal, ever-contemporary appropriateness and relevance of the grand themes explored in biblical stories. They say that the enduring relevance of the ancient stories derives from the way they have resonated with the everyday experiences of men and women seeking to survive purposefully in God's world. To take these themes as the basis for the backstory lines of a television animation series, set in a real situation, at a real time in history, would seem to use both the medium and the message in an excitingly relevant way.

This symbolically marks the final shift from the hesitant explorations with a new model in the early days of the first pilot. The centrality of the story of the story-tellers; the interaction of the biblical stories they preserve and retell as part of their home and community lives at times of great pressure; the greater concentration on the personalities and characteristics of the central characters who carry the story and their development: these mark a major change from the early days. The contextual model has developed beyond the anonymous voice-over story-teller and the sketchily drawn background situation of the early days. The developed model is now equally influenced by the style of children's Saturday morning television and the soap opera. This means that, in addition to exciting adventures, far more detailed characters and storylines are being created.

We have moved a long way from the prettily presented Sunday School Bible story told simply by a voice-over. We are moving out of the ghetto in which we have been protected for so long into territory more normally occupied by mass entertainment shows. We are swimming in new waters for the religious broadcaster. So far we have steered clear of the rocks and sharks, although so far we have not ventured far from the shallow, well-protected waters of the reserved slots and the Christian video marketplace in which we swam for so long. It is tempting to swim back or to remain in touching distance of the safety of the bank. But that would be illusory.

Winding up a previewing of *The Story Keepers* at a meeting of members of Churches Together in England, the General Secretary, the Rev. Martin Reardon, told the press and members of the meeting: 'I certainly didn't think when I was teaching theological students that, twenty years later, what I was telling them about New Testament scholarship would end up as the basis of a children's cartoon!' I smiled and remembered the words of my mentor Alan Dale, repeated as often to his junior colleagues as to his teacher training students, 'Never be afraid of scholarship!' His mantra was usually preceded by an attack on teachers and clergy who took biblical scholarship seriously in the privacy of their own study but who left everything behind when they were faced with a group of eager children, finding it more comfortable to fall back on simplistic platitudes and pious moralisms. Alan was right in the 1960s to urge teachers to use the findings of scholarship in their teaching of the Bible in the classroom. *The Story Keepers* has shown that the axiom is equally right for religious broadcasters 40 years later. Even if the pressures of ratings demand that we entertain and hold mass audiences as well as educate them, broadcasters have a duty to ensure that the content of programming, particularly for young audiences, is as accurate and true to the findings of scholarship as it can be. Even if we are only producing biblical animated cartoons.

When the Archbishop of Canterbury complimented me on the professionalism of the final product of *The Story Keepers*, I thought to myself: 'So it should be. It cost over $5 million.' The Archbishop added that, amid so much Christian television for children that was characterised by cheap, amateurish production values, *The Story Keepers* was rare. I said nothing then, and have been reluctant to say anything since, about the additional personal cost to myself and my family, of raising the money to make the series possible – surviving all the ups and downs of remortgaging our house twice, struggling until long after the series was a success to repay the loan and free our house from a bank charge. Nor have I spoken of the personal struggle in the face of those who regarded me as slightly potty, and called the whole enterprise 'Brown's Folly'.

Those, however, are the costs involved in rejecting the amateur way and never being satisfied with less than the very best for the Highest, as my Non-Conformist forbears would have put it. If the success of *The Story Keepers* teaches anything, it is that the only way to compete is on the same terms as all broadcasters, never being satisfied with anything but the highest production values, even if that might mean years of struggle to get it right, and far more money to create than is normally available for religious broadcast shows.

Finally, what I have learned is that, no matter how dogged one's resolution to hold on to the bitter end, there must be an over-riding concept worth holding on to. One American producer, the dollar signs flashing in his eyes, summed up the essence of the ongoing temptation before anyone who, like me, has what appears to be a commercially profitable notion: 'That's a sure winner,' he said. 'That story has been around a long time.' You can't miss, he was saying. It will make itself. It was constantly tempting to be seduced by such thinking, and to deviate from the hard slog of revision, rewrite and rethink necessary to ensure the concept not only was honed but was held on to at all times.

My colleagues on the team talked frequently of 'Brian's Vision'. I like to think that the whole project was and remains that: a Vision whose realisation I have been privileged to be part of. It began to be fulfilled on that Sunday morning in January 1997. I hope I shall see its continued fulfilment in the new millennium.

Epilogue
Principalities and powers:
Another contemporary parable

The period after evening supper on Monday evenings, or 'tables' as it was called in the Methodist theological college in the late 1950s, was devoted to reports, usually humorous, of incidents in services conducted by the student ministers the day before.

'I leaned across the pulpit,' reported the preacher. 'I looked the congregation in the eye. Then I said: "In common with most theologians and ministers today, I do not believe in a personal devil." Before I could utter another word an old boy in the front replied: "Ay. But we do. And so do 'e." '

The student's embarrassment was the subject of popular humour for the rest of the term. It was dismissed as typical of what to expect in the Black Country. I joined the fun.

As a lecturer in religious studies I prided myself on my academic objectivity and the dexterity with which I refused to be drawn one way or the other on the subject of the existence of a power of evil in opposition to the power of God in the world. I would warn my students to steer wide of the conspiracy theories of certain evangelical writers, above all those who drew concerned attention to the electronic media as the battleground in which demonic powers were at work. I distanced myself as a

teacher of theology from theories which saw diabolic, malign in-
fluences in bar codes and in personal computers.

Later, as a media researcher, I aligned myself with those in the
churches and research groups who called for balance and clear
heads in the face of the moral panics and hysteria whipped up in
the press and Parliament about the evil social effects of the
so-called 'video nasties'. I found it hard to attribute such evil to
the work of a personal power, or to see the efforts to control
availability of the videos as part of an ongoing battle between the
powers of good and the powers of evil. I could not see the new
electronic media as a battleground in the ongoing struggle for
cosmic supremacy between the forces of Light and the Prince of
Darkness.

That was until I began my quest to take the story of Jesus to
those untouched by the churches, going outside the normal
channels and using broadcast television. As I look back on the
events of the past ten years I see the hand of what I call 'divine
serendipity' at work. I see also a series of events and encounters
which could equally be attributed to demonic coincidence: the
number of financial institutions which crashed within weeks of
becoming involved with the project; the businesses, professional
as well as commercial, which failed or were taken over soon after
becoming associated with the project; the media organisations
which once worked with the project and which have since
disappeared; the studios which went bankrupt; the confidence
tricksters; the charlatans and, worse, the church-going financial
dealers who openly parade their Christian commitment yet
engage in dubious business activities; the stress and strain; the
illness and pain.

As I look back now I can understand the arguments of those
who say that these all seem to point to the activity of a personal
power of evil, determined to thwart and disrupt an attempt to
reach those whom he regards as his private constituency. After
all, he has had it his own way until now. He is happy with
the way things are. He is content with the ineffectiveness of

traditional modes. They are harmless and easily ignored. They confirm the Christian story as outmoded and Christians as tired and defeated. But reaching 49 per cent of all 4-to-9-year-olds watching British television on a Sunday morning, at a time when those belonging to Sunday Schools and Junior Churches were in church – that is war. And not one which the powers of evil are winning.

Or am I falling for another conspiracy theory?

Appendix

The evolution of a concept, 1970–95

(a) 1970: The idea is formed

Chapter 5 of the author's workbook, *The Choice* (Denholm House/E. J. Arnold, 1970)

The Sign of the Fish   A Play

Five Voices, Host, Silas.

Host: It's just Silas we are waiting for. He knows we are
               meeting here, I suppose?
1st Voice: I saw him last night near the Coliseum. I reminded
               him of the service.

Host: He's new. Does he know the sign to look for?

1st Voice: I told him the street and said look for the door post chalked with a fish. He said he understood.

2nd Voice: I hope he turns up. If the police see the fish, we're done for.

1st Voice: I told him to be on time. (*Noise off*) What was that? (*Pause*) It's Silas. I can see him. He's rubbing out the chalk mark. We are safe now.

Host: Make a place for him round the table.... (*Enter Silas*) Ah! Come in Silas! Welcome to our meeting. We were just beginning to get anxious.

Silas: So was I. The police are everywhere.

2nd Voice: Did they see you? We can't take the risk.

3rd Voice: If you ask me it's getting too hot. I don't like it. They'll find us before long, you mark my words.

2nd Voice: You're right. Every time that door opens I'm sure it's the end.

Silas: I wouldn't have come...

Host: Nonsense! You're welcome. But they're right. It is risky. Some of our friends are meeting in the caves below the city. If it gets too dangerous, we may have to as well.

4th Voice: We have as much right to services as anyone else. If anyone tries to stop me, he'll feel the end of my sword.

5th Voice: What a lot of cowards you are! I'm not frightened by threats from the Emperor. It'll take more than a few soldiers to make me go underground.

4th Voice: There's enough of us. The Jews used not to stand for it. Even Pontius Pilate couldn't keep them down. Didn't Peter once talk about the Zealots and the guerillas? There are more of us. Those Jews make us look feeble.

5th Voice: I don't care about death. They won't frighten me. I say, we've got to fight for our rights. The only way we shall be free to meet and have services is if we show them that we won't be bullied.

4th Voice: Hear! Hear! I've had enough of running away. We've been hounded and harried for months. Meeting in secret. Scared every time the door opens. Frightened every time we get home, in case the police are waiting. I can't stand any more. Nor can my family. It's time for a show-down.

5th Voice: They've been asking for it.

Host: Friends! Listen to me. I'm an old man. You have your lives to live. Mine is nearly over. I know you are anxious. We all are. The Emperor and his guards are making it unpleasant for us all. But this is not the way. This is not what we learned from Peter, Paul and the friends of Jesus. My father used to talk about Peter. Just like you, he was: hot-headed and violent.

5th Voice: But...

2nd Voice: Shush, Paulinus; listen to Servius.

Host: He used to admit that he never understood Jesus. Funny chap. He was so ashamed of the way he let Jesus down that when his turn came and they arrested him and took him out to crucify him, Peter asked them to nail him upside down on the cross. Couldn't bring himself to die the same way as Jesus, you see.

4th Voice: I can't see what that's got to do with us.

Host: I didn't think you would, or else you wouldn't talk the way you do about the police. Why do you think Mark is writing down the stories of Jesus which Peter told? So that people like us can hear what Jesus did and what he said.

1st Voice: Every time the knock comes on the door I think of
                   what Jesus did when they came to arrest him. I
                   remember the story Peter told us. I bet he was the
                   one who drew his sword.

> "We were in the garden with Jesus when we
> saw a band of men coming, armed with clubs
> and swords. They were being led by Judas and
> he walked up to Jesus and kissed him. Then
> these men grabbed Jesus and put him under
> guard. There was a man standing nearby who
> drew his sword and cut off the ear of a Jewish
> officer. That caused quite a stir. But Jesus
> promptly healed the soldier, so that was the end
> of that. Then Jesus asked them why they should
> come out armed and take him like a bandit
> when he had been teaching quite openly in the
> Temple. But this, of course, was what the Bible
> said would happen!"

Do you remember this story? There was some
action in that.

Host: But it was Judas I felt sorry for. Was he so different
                   from the other friends that Jesus had? I bet Peter,
                   John and James were as surprised as Judas when
                   Jesus befriended the Roman centurion and healed
                   his servant.

1st Voice: And there was that time in the Temple courtyard
                   when the Jewish leaders tried to trap him by asking
                   him whether it was right to pay taxes to the
                   Roman emperor, or not. His friends didn't
                   expect him to say, "Give what belongs to the
                   Emperor back to him, and give what is God's back
                   to God."

Host: It's easy to say that Judas did not understand Jesus. None of his disciples understood. Even when Jesus told them the Romans would kill him and that he would come back because his death would not be the end, for he would soon rise. Peter admitted that even then they did not understand.

2nd Voice: Jesus did not hate them like you want us to. He did what he told us to do. Do you remember? I think he said, "To the man who hits you on the cheek give him the other cheek to hit." And when he was dying on the cross he said, "Father, forgive them. They know not what they do." I've heard that the Roman officer in charge of the guard was standing facing Jesus and saw how he died. He said, "This man was a real king."

Silence . . .

(b) 1989: An idea developed

Extracts from a memorandum to the advisers to *The Choice* animation project and a memorandum to John Halas, outlining the contextual approach for the first time

Flame Communications Ltd.

1, CUMMINGS CLOSE,
HEADINGTON,
OXFORD. OX3 8ND.

Telephone (0865) 750893.
12th February 1989

<u>Memorandum to advisers</u>
Anita Beer
Angelo Colacrai
Dr Cyril Rodd
Rev Prof Daniel Hardy
Prof James Dunn
Rev Prof Frances Young
Rev Noel Vincent
Rev Julia Neuberger
Rev Hans Florin
John Halas
<u>From Brian Brown</u>

The Choice

Enclosed please find a) the first drafts of the first five storyboards.
　　　　　　　　　　 b) the first drafts of the scripts of the series. You will
　　　　　　　　　　　　 receive the complete set of 50 scripts in the next few
　　　　　　　　　　　　 days.

1. The following notes of explanation outline the principles upon which the
   series has been based. They should be read alongside other previously
   circulated material. Please consider them and respond to the following 2
   questions.
   a) How far are the principles acceptable for a television series of this
      nature in your view?
   b) How far in your view are the individual scripts in line with them?
2. Please note the stages of production:
   1. The scripts containing voice-over commentary in the right hand
      column and suggestions for visuals in the accompanying panels have
      to be agreed for content, vocabulary, style. A meeting is to be held in
      London on March 9th chaired by Noel Vincent. Any comments
      advisers have about the principles outlined in the accompanying notes
      or any other general comment at this stage will be valued.
   2. The storyboard, containing voice-over commentary and illustrations is
      then agreed.
   3. The animation is created on the basis of the storyboard.

Registered in England FLAME COMMUNICATIONS Ltd. Reg. No. 2243021

5. As far as possible the scripts try not to mix traditions in one episode. There are exceptions to the general rule eg. the reference in the narrative of the feeding of the 5,000 men to their trying to make Jesus a king from John. This is kept to a minimum however.
6. All references to Jesus, the Jews and Sabbath-breaking are omitted on the grounds that the incidents though of interest to the Early Church contain concepts beyond the interest and the comprehension of most of the target audience particularly the young.
7. Following the pattern established in New World an attempt is made to present material in the earliest orally circulated forms and those verses regarded by some scholars as Church-words or later accretions are omitted.

Style of presentation

1. The thrust of the presentation is that the stories were first preserved and circulated in oral form, repeated at informal and more formal meetings of Christians and re-told to respond to or provoked by certain situations. The series focuses on groups of Christians meeting in Rome in homes and secret places during the persecutions in the weeks prior to the death of Peter which may have prompted the writing down of the stories. What the programmes are doing imaginatively is putting a camera into a group and eavesdropping.

2. 2 storylines run parallel:
   a) the story-telling community during a period of severe persecution; fear, their courage, bravery and motivation for preserving and telling the story.
   b) the stories they told about Jesus and remembered of what he said, all placed contextually in 1st century Rome and Palestine in the days of Jesus.

This story-telling style enables us to deal with certain problems without necessarily losing the essential balance of traditional and more liberal stances.

Memo to: John Halas
From: Brian Brown
cc all advisers

The Choice

Perspective from which voice-over script written.

1. The Biblical and Theological advisers are agreed that recognition should
   be given to the following:
   a) The gospel stories were preserved by word of mouth in the Christian
      communities. They were not written down until almost 40 years after
      the death of Jesus. During that time the stories were passed on in
      group meetings and handed on firstly by those who were living eye-
      witnesses and then by others who heard the stories from these wit-
      nesses. For this reason it is suggested that the stories be set in a
      community in Rome at the time of the Neronic persecution during
      which Peter and Paul probably lost their lives. The stories in the series
      would be presented as though they were being re-told verbally in a
      group meeting behind closed doors passing on the stories in the pe-
      riod prior to their being written down.
   b) What was being re-told were real stories about a real man living in a
      real situation. This situation was dominated for the Jews, from whom
      Jesus came, by the hatred and privation caused by the Roman occu-
      pation of Palestine and by the unrest caused by the Resistance move-
      ment which operated against the Romans and their Jewish quisling
      collaborators, the tax gatherers and toll gate keepers.
   c) Jesus faced real choices as a prophet and preacher. But he could not
      avoid his human limitations despite his special powers.

2. So, the 2 draft commentaries you have seen and the ones I am currently
   working on give due recognition to the stories being handed on, but also
   that they took place in a real political situation.

(c) 1990: *The Choice*

**Voice-over of the pilot by Robin Lyons,
and storyboards by John Halas**

THE CHOICE

Opening sequence at the beginning of each episode.

Words superimposed and rolling over a scene of the city of Rome in raging fire.

Voice reading the words.

STORYTELLER

It is AD 64 and Rome is on fire.

And who does the Emperor Nero blame for it?

Us. The Christians.

We have to run from his soldiers,
hide away from his anger.

But when we see the sign of the fish
we know we are with friends.

And safe in secret places beneath the city
we can comfort each other with stories about
our leader . . .

Jesus.

(d) 1992: *The Story*

Extracts from the first hand-written draft, May 1992, and Draft 1, June 1992

<u>DIALOGUE</u>   5

Helen   ~~Finish~~.

* ☐ 6. The guards are gone. You will sleep here tonight, but you must keep quiet.

Marcus

7. Finish that story about Jesus uncle Ben.

Helen

8. ~~He has~~ Uncle Ben ~~to make~~ bread for the morning
   I'll tell you my favourite story about Jesus.
   It's a story told after he was grown up, but it's about when he was very little
   Of course none of us were there when he was little

9. But now he is no longer with us this story is special
   It means a lot to us now.

Helen

10. There is a town in Palestine, not far from where your uncle Ben grew up. It's called Nazareth.

13. A man called Joseph and a girl called Mary lived there.

14. They were waiting to get married.

Nazareth is only a small town. Palestine is only a small country

15. ~~They couldn't them~~ ~~It is~~ It is part of our Empire now
    Uncle Ben will tell you the people there hated being ruled by the Emperor

They long to be free, They dream of the day
                    them
God will send a great leader.

17. Some of them prepared to fight.
18. Others like Mary prayed.

DIALOGUE
HELEN

6. The Guards are gone. You will sleep here tonight. But you must keep quiet.

MARCUS

7. Finish that story about Jesus uncle Ben.

HELEN

8. Uncle Ben has to bake bread for the morning.
I'll tell you my favourite story about Jesus.
It's a story told after he was grown up, but it's about when he was very little.
Of course none of us were there when he was little.

9. But now he is no longer with us this story is special. It means a lot to us now.

HELEN

10. There is a town in Palestine, not far from where your uncle Ben grew up. It's called Nazareth.

13. A man called Joseph and a girl called Mary lived there.

14. They were waiting to get married.
Nazareth is only a small town. Palestine is only a small country.

15. It is part of our Empire now.
Uncle Ben will tell you the people there hated being ruled by the Emperor.
They long to be free. They dream of the day
God will send them a great leader.

17. Some of them prepared to fight.

18. Others like Mary prayed.

DIALOGUE

Angel

19. Shalom – Peace be with you. The Lord has blessed you and is with you

Helen.

20. Mary was confused and wondered what it meant.

Angel

God is pleased with you. You will have a son and will call him
Jesus. ~~~~~~~~~~~~~~~~~~~~~~~

Helen.

~~The angel~~ He said he would be the one the people were looking for

Mary.

21. How can this happen?

Angel

There is nothing God cannot do. His spirit will come to you
and his power will rest on you.

~~The baby~~   Angel

The child will be a holy child. He will be called the
son of God.

Mary

22. I am the Lord's servant. Let it happen to me as you have
said.

Helen.

~~Everything happened just as the~~
Then it happened. Mary learned she was indeed going to have
a baby

24. Because they weren't ~~married~~ Joseph thought the right thing ~~to do was to break off~~ ~~the wedding~~ their ~~~~ quietly.

But he had a dream

Angel

26. Don't be afraid to marry Mary. Her baby is to come from
God. You will have a son. You shall call him Jesus
because he will save his people from their sins.

Helen.

27. When he awoke Joseph immediately ~~married Mary~~ decided to go ahead
with the wedding as
planned.

DIALOGUE

ANGEL

19. Shalom – Peace be with you. The Lord has blessed you and is with you.

HELEN

20. Mary was confused and wondered what it meant.

ANGEL

God is with you. You will have a son and will call him Jesus.

HELEN

He said he would be the one the people were looking for.

MARY

21. How can this happen?

ANGEL

There is nothing God cannot do. His spirit will come to you and his power will rest on you.

ANGEL

The child will be a holy child. He will be called the son of God.

MARY

23. I am the Lord's servant. Let it happen to me as you have said

HELEN

Then it happened. Mary learned she was indeed going to have a baby.

25. Because they were not married Joseph thought the right thing to do was to break off the engagement there and then quietly. But he had a dream.

ANGEL

26. Don't be afraid to marry Mary. Her baby is to come from God. You will have a son. You shall call him Jesus because he will save his people from their sins.

HELEN

27. When he awoke Joseph immediately decided to go ahead with the wedding as planned.

DRAFT 1	*THE STORY*
Episode 1	Opening shot – A.D. 64, some indication that location is Rome.
	Roman Guard holding imperial standard with eagle on top.
	Flames begin to appear from town.
	Soldier and standard merge into the flame.
	The eagle flies up from the standard and hovers above the city, wings outspread casting dark shadow.
	Shadow over city in flames; through houses, through streets, orchards.
NURSE: Lullaby	Nurse holding baby emerges from the shadows standing in a doorway watching as flames engulf houses.
	People fleeing.
	Attempts to douse fires with water.
	With brooms; beating with mats.
	Woman singing lullaby to the baby.
	Roman soldiers/guards marching towards a house in the street.
	Nurse watches.
	Nurse slips around the corner.
	3 children, 2 boys, 7 and 4, 1 girl, 4, being hurried out of back/side exit.
MOTHER (*VO*): Find the house with this on it.	Mother unseen; only hands and arms.
	Hands of mother drawing sign of the fish in the dust of the road.
	Children looking for the house.
	Street after street.
	Nurse follows at a distance.
	Hurrying along: little one being dragged.

Turn a corner.

See a group of soldiers outside the bakers holding empty baskets.

Children quickly hide and look around corner.

Baker fills baskets with fresh bread, cakes etc.

Baker laughs.

Soldiers turn and walk off down the road.

(*Long shot*): children head round corner, see soldiers disappearing.

Baker sees them go, looks left, right.

Baker draws sign of the fish in flour on the door.

JUSTIN: (*Lip Sync*): It's Uncle Ben, the storyteller.

Justin pointing to house door.

(*C Up*) Justin (7yr old boy) looking surprised.

MARCUS: (*Lip Sync*): I wonder if he's got any cake?

(*C Up*) Marcus.

Children creep cautiously to the door followed by the nurse at a distance.

Justin knocks on the door.

Door opened by woman.

HELENA: (*Lip sync*): Ben Ami! It is the children!

(*C Up*) Helena

BEN: (*VO*) I'm kneading the dough. Now why do we knead the dough?

(*C Up*) (*Lip sync*) Ben – Face.

ALL CHILDREN CHANT IN UNISON: Because everyone needs the bread.

Notes

(*VO*) = Voice-over   (*C Up*) = Close-up

(e) 1993: Almost there

The three-minute promotional video

A Roman centurion stands against the stark background of a burning city. An eagle on his arm takes off and soars majestically over the flames and smoke as dramatic music announces the scenes of horror to come. As the eagle hovers the camera zooms down to the blazing streets below.

The voice-over announces that the Emperor Nero has set fire to the city.

Citizens are fighting the fire in desperation. We see soldiers banging on doors. The voice-over tells us that they are searching for Christians, causing them to flee their homes in panic.

We see people fleeing and a mother kneeling in the road outside her house. She is bidding a tearful farewell to a girl and her two brothers. The woman is drawing a fish with her fingers in the dust. That is the sign that the children are to look for. She points them in the right direction as she goes inside to wait arrest.

The voice-over introduces the children who we see dodging the soldiers. We see Anna, Justin and Marcus hiding around the corner of a baker's shop.

The baker's name, we are told, is Ben. He is famous all over Rome for his cakes and pastries.

We see the fat jolly baker bid farewell to a customer. He looks around and seeing that all is clear he chalks a fish (the same Ichthus sign that the mother drew in the dust) on his door.

The children glance at each other, recognising the sign. They knock on the door and are welcomed in by a jolly looking woman. We cut to the bakery where we see Ben entertaining the children with his party tricks of tossing dough and making dough animals whilst the children, particularly the youngest, look on with delight in their eyes.

His cakes and bread make him popular with children. But the voice-over tells us that he is even more famous for his storytelling.

As we cut to Jesus talking to his disciples the voice-over informs us that Ben tells the children about another storyteller . . . the one from Nazareth called Jesus.

Stills of Jesus calming the storm, the shepherd with his sheep, the returning prodigal, John baptising Jesus, Jesus and the blind man, the three crosses at Golgotha and two more animated sequences of Jesus lifting a child and gazing over the city in a gentle breeze provide illustrations of the stories that Ben will tell.

The voice-over tells us that these stories are the story of the journeys Jesus made. They are told in thirteen half hour episodes which will live in our hearts for generations.

(f) 1994: The concept complete

The 90-second introduction to
The Story Keepers

Intended to catch the attention at the beginning of each episode this series of sequences with a dramatic, aggressive voice-over follows closely the pattern of the three minute promotional video produced two years earlier. The promo was designed to catch the attention of television buyers at the international markets. The 90 second introduction was aimed at general television and video viewing audiences.

The 90 second introduction is more attention grabbing but uses much of the same animation created for the earlier piece. It too begins with the soldier, the eagle, the flaming background, the burning city, the desperate fire fighting and the fleeing, panicking populace. But it adds the period establishing voice-over . . . 'Rome, 64 AD'.

Focus is placed upon the terror and the persecution of the Christians and upon one man . . . the Emperor Nero, who has unleashed his fury against the followers of Jesus. He has, says the voice-over, separated families, left children homeless and thrown hundreds of Christians to the lions or forced them into slavery.

Then, just as in the promo, but this time through a collage of sequences from the series itself, we are introduced to the main characters: Anna, Justin, Marcus and their friend Cyrus, who we see dodging the advancing soldiers as they search in vain for their missing parents.

Then we meet Ben, the local baker, and his wife Helena who we are told rescue the children and introduce them to the Christian underground.

We learn that Ben and Helena are part of a network of brave men and women with a mission who risk their lives to keep the stories of Jesus alive.

And *The Story Keepers* had begun.

(g) 1994: The Biblical content of *The Story*

The Story

Biblical Content
by Brian Brown

1. Three to four stories per 22-minute episode.

2. Stories represent the kerygma of the early church in Rome in AD 64,
    and incorporate the theme of Mark's gospel. Mark was preserving the
    kerygma. Ben would have been keeping it alive.

3. Structure of kerygma.
    Parables: Stories proclaiming Jesus as the:
    > Healer
    > Teacher
    > Miracle Worker
    > Suffering Servant

    demonstrating his:
    > POWER over nature and evil
    > POWER over sickness
    > POWER over death.

4   Perspective of the kerygma.
    Seen through the resurrection.
    Focal point the resurrection.

    Proposed grouping of the stories:

    > Nativity stories: (not kerygma, not part of the Rome message. Ben
    > part of his tradition for broadcasting reasons expected.)

    > Events and teachings: Encounters in Galilee, taking place at
    > different times and places in no special order, showing who Jesus
    > is by demonstrating his charisma and power.

    > Passion Stories: A coherent block of stories which by this time
    > were kept together for teaching and pastoral purposes. They were
    > told regularly around the table when Christians gathered in homes,
    > and in the catacombs, to remind them of the salvation events
    > leading to the crucifixion, and to the final demonstration of the
    > power in the person of Jesus as recorded in the resurrection
    > narratives, and beyond.

The Story
Stories considered essential by Advisors

Item	The Story Screenplay Draft 2	Biblical References
(Episode 1)		
Nature Miracle Stories		
The feeding of the 5000	pp. 115–120	Mk 6:31–46
Stilling of the storm	pp. 85–89	Mk 4:35–41
Walking on water		Mk 6:47–55
Healing Miracle Stories		
Healing of 'Legion'	pp. 81–84	Mk 5:1–20
(Episode 2)		
John the Baptist/Baptism of Jesus	pp. 44–47	Mk 1:1–13
Zacchaeus	pp. 92–95	Lk 19:1–10
Jairus' daughter	pp. 65–69	Mk 5:21–43
(Episode 3)		
Suffer little children come to me	pp. 174–176	Mk 9:33–37
Parable: The Sower	pp. 76–78	Mk 4:3–8
Unforgiving Servant	pp. 157–159	Matt 18:25–34
(Episode 4)		
Parable: The Lost Coin		
Parable: The Lost Sheep	pp. 292–294	
Parable: The Prodigal Son	pp. 101–108	Lk 15:11–32
(Episode 5)		
Nativity Stories	pp. 8–27	Lk 1:26–38
		Matt 1:18–24
		Lk 2:1–7, 8–21
		Matt 2:1–12, 13–23
(Episode 6)		
Centurion's servant	pp. 12–125	Lk 7:1–10
Parable: The good Samaritan	pp. 109–113	Lk 10:30–36
The paralytic (Jesus tells House on Sand parable at start)	pp. 71–73	Mk 2:3–12
(Episode 7)		
Man with withered hand	pp. 132–135	Lk 13:10–16
Deaf and dumb man	pp. 140–141	Mk 7:32–37
Blind man	pp. 142–143	Mk 8:22–26
Epileptic boy	pp. 152–154	Mk 9:14–27

Item	The Story Screenplay Draft 2	Biblical References
(Episode 8)		
Thankfulness		
Syro-Phoenician woman's daughter	pp. 162–163	Mk 7:25–30
Lepers	pp. 163–165	Lk 17:11–19
(Unforgiving Servant)	pp. 157–159	Matt 18:25–34
Blind Bartimaeus	pp. 177–179	Mk 10:48–52
(Passion A)		
Transfiguration	pp. 149–151	Mk 9:2–10
The Last Week		
Entry into Jerusalem	pp. 188–191	Mk 11:1–11
Overturning the tables	pp. 194–196	Mk 11:15–19
(Taxes to Caesar)	pp. 198–199	Mk 12:13–17
(Widow's mite)	pp. 200–201	Mk 12:41–44
(Passion B)		
Jesus is betrayed by Judas	pp. 204–206 & 216	Mk 14:1–2, 10–11
Anointing of Jesus	pp. 205/6–208	Mk 14:3–9
Preparing for the Last Supper	pp. 209–210	Mk 14:12–16
Washing the feet of the disciples	pp. 211–212	John 13:1, 4–5, 12, 15–17
Last Supper	pp. 217–219	Mk 14:17–25
(Passion C)		
Jesus forecasts Peter's betrayal	pp. 220	Mk 14:26–31
Gethsemane, the arrest of Jesus	pp. 224–227	Mk 14:32–52
The trials of Jesus, Peter's denial	pp. 229–234	Mk 14:53–72
(Passion D)		
Trial before Pilate	pp. 234–240	Mk 15:1–15
Crucifixion	pp. 244–250	Mk 15:21–41
The burial with promise of resurrection	pp. 251–253	Mk 15:42–47
(Easter Passion)		
Resurrection Narratives		
In the garden	pp. 255–260	Lk 24:1–11
Road to Emmaus	pp. 261–264	Lk 24:13–35
The upper room	pp. 265/267–269	Lk 24:36–53
On the shore	pp. 270–273	
Ascension	pp. 279–280	Acts 1:6–14
Pentecost	pp. 285–289	Acts 2:1–41

The Complete Story Keepers Collection

1-85608-395-0

Chasing breathless through tunnels under
ancient Rome ...

Battling with baddies on an enemy slave ship ...

Wild adventures and daring rescues abound as
Ben the Baker's orphan friends risk everything
to keep the stories of Jesus alive.

Wicked Nero wants to feed them to the lions.
Nasty Nihilus is after their blood. But no power
on earth can stop ...

The Storykeepers

COMING EARLY 2001

Three new Story Keepers Books

Story Keepers At Risk

Story Keepers In Danger

Story Keepers In A Struggle

The Story Keepers Video Selection

The Christmas Story Keepers
VA30713
Running time: 70 minutes
The first seventy-minute feature film in the Story Keeper series, with songs, sadness, stories and the Christmas story for the whole family. The Christmas Story Keepers is as timeless as the nativity story itself! Already shown on TV, your family will watch this video time and again.

The Easter Story Keepers
VA30710
Running time: 70 minutes
An exciting video suitable for all ages 4 and over. Bursting with energy, and packed with gripping action the telling of the Easter story is cleverly woven into the life of the early Christians. Helena, Cyrus, Justin and Marcus manage to escape Nihilus' attempts to burn them out of the bakery, but it leads to Ben, Justin and Marcus getting arrested in the catacombs under the city ... but this is just the start! An all-year-round must for home, school, Sunday school and ...

The Story Keepers Video Selection

Breakout and Raging Waters
VA30703 – Running time: 50 minutes

Catacomb Rescue and Ready Aim Fire
VA30704 – Running time: 48 minutes

Sink or Swim and Road in the Night
VA30705 – Running time: 50 minutes

Captured and Trapped
VA30706 - Running time: 50 minutes

Tricked by a Traitor and Tried and True
VA30707 – Running time: 48 minutes

**Caught at the Crossroads and
To the Ends of the Earth**
VA30708 – Running time: 48 minutes

Starlight Escape
VA30709 – Running time: 25 minutes